HEALING
RELATIONSHIPS

by
Serge Kahili King

First English edition 2006
ISBN #1-890850-21-7

Published by
Hunaworks
PO Box 223009
Princeville HI 96722

ACKNOWLEDGMENTS

I would like to acknowledge and give thanks to all those who helped me to write this book, including my parents, Harry and Joyce; my great-grandparents and grandparents; my brothers Harry, Loring, and Darrel; my sisters Dee and Marilyn; my awesome wife Gloria; our children Chris, Pierre, and Dion; my extended family of relatives that includes aunts and uncles and cousins, nieces and nephews, in-laws and grandchildren; my Hawaiian family and my Aloha International 'ohana; my students and friends all over the world; and even those few who have decided that they don't like me at all. Thank you all for being my teachers.

TABLE OF CONTENTS

PART ONE

The Fundamentals

CHAPTER ONE
RELATIONSHIP BASICS

In old Hawaii there were many legends of how things came to be. Here is one from the Kahili family of Kauai.

In a time before time, in a place where there were no places, there was Kumulipo, the deep, dark, profound and mysterious void. In that infinite emptiness was an infinite potential waiting to be filled, but unable to manifest because of the tension between two forces: Wakea, the male force of Chaos, and Papa, the female force of Order.

At some timeless point the tension gave way. Chaotic movement interacted with Orderly stillness to form the First Wave. Out of that First Wave was manifested the First Relationship. And there's been Trouble ever since.

Why People Relate

Waves exist because of a relationship between movement and stillness, and everything exists in a multitude of relationships with other things. Not all relationships are healthy, however, in terms of being beneficial to whomever or whatever is related. This is especially true of human relationships, the subject of this particular book. Considering all the differences between men and women, between men and men, between women and women, between cultures and environments and everything else, it is a mystery and a wonder that anyone ever gets along with anyone else.

And yet, they do. Most people, most of the time, do get along, lots of people, some of the time, don't, and a few people all of the time never do. This book is primarily for the second group.

What's really amazing is that so many people do figure out how to get along all by themselves, without any help. What's so sad is that so many people don't know how to do it, for whatever reason. Leaving out the people who just don't want to get along with others, I think that everyone who wants to get along can do so, because I believe that, fundamentally, everyone does want to get along. I also believe that all it takes is some simple knowledge of what to do, and how to do it.

If we want to understand relationships, then we have to understand why people want to relate in the first place. People don't do anything without a good reason, especially something as difficult as establishing and maintaining a good relationship with someone else. So what kind of reason could people have that is compelling enough for them to undertake something as difficult as relating to another human being?

The answer lies in what motivates people to do anything at all, from getting up in the morning, to relating and working and playing during the day, to going to bed at night. All human behavior is rooted in something so fundamental that it is usually overlooked. I am reminded of a very old joke about a man who is standing on a street corner, hitting himself on the head with a hammer. When another man asks him why he is doing that, the first man says, "Because it feels so good when I stop." Everybody, really, just wants to feel good. It's as simple as that.

People get up in the morning when it feels better than lying in bed. People go to work when work itself, or some benefit provided by work (like food, shelter, or clothing), makes them feel better than they would without it. People play games when such play makes them feel good, or when playing gives them something else which makes them feel good, like money, health, or praise. People go to bed at night when that makes them feel better than not going to bed. And people relate to other people, go out of their way to find people to relate to, put up with all kinds of inconveniences, difficulties, and dangers in order to relate to other people, when relating makes them feel better than not relating.

That's all well and good, you may say (and I've just said it for those of you who didn't think about saying it), but it seems too general to be very useful. Well, you are right, so let's look more closely at what makes people feel good.

What Is "Feeling Good?"

Before discussing what makes people feel good, we ought to examine what "feeling good" really means.

Basically, this is a physiological sensation of pleasure. Even when you feel good because you've solved a problem in arithmetic (or algebra, or geometry, or calculus, or a cross-word puzzle, etc.), there is a physiological response that we interpret as pleasure. Like it or not, the body is always involved in any experience of feeling good, whether we associate the experience with our body, our mind, or our spirit.

The actual sensation of feeling good comes from a sudden release of physical tension. A small release of tension produces a small sensation of pleasure, and a large release of tension produces a large sensation of pleasure. Sometimes, however, a sudden release of tension produces a sudden increase of tension, which we call fear or anger, but otherwise

4

the tension release just feels good.

As to what causes the sudden release of tension, one common element in many experiences is sudden change. I remember reading a report by a marketing firm in the United States which stated that retailers could generally count on a significant increase in shoppers right after any change in the weather. According to the report, it didn't matter whether the weather changed from sunny to rainy or rainy to sunny. In either case the number of shoppers would increase. The sudden change in weather released tension in people, which led to increased activity.

To relate this to relationships, one of the sources of pleasure experienced in a relationship with another person has to do with the amount and frequency of tension release provided by the relationship. Sexual activity will immediately come to mind for many people, but that is only one of a great many opportunities for tension release, and therefore feeling good, in all relationships.

Another common element in many pleasurable experiences involving the sudden release of tension is based on the engagement of familiar patterns. There is an old saying in English that "familiarity breeds contempt," meaning that the more familiar something or someone is, the less importance and respect it receives. However, this is only valid when the familiar thing or person stimulates resistance, i.e., tension. Much more often, "familiarity breeds pleasure." Thus the pleasure we derive from hobbies, holidays, games whose rules we know well, playing music, dancing, and, when there is no reason for resistance, encounters with beloved family members and old friends. Experiencing familiar people, places, things, and habits provides a sense of security, accompanied by a release of tension, and that feels good.

Differences And Similarities

Someone sent me an anonymous quote that I like a lot: "Men are from Earth, women are from Earth. Deal with it."

It may be useful and amusing to look at the differences between men and women in how they behave and think. Some of this is due to physiology, of course, but most of it is due to culture. Many differences that are valid in one society may not apply at all in another one.

In one book on differences, the authors assert that there are primary differences in men and women because of hundreds of thousands of years of evolution. Brain structure, according to them, is why men are naturally polygamous and women monogamous, male groups have leaders and female groups are cooperative, men like to work and women like to talk, men are hunters and women are caregivers, and so on. Such an assertion blithely ignores societies with polygamous women or monogamous men, female leaders and male cooperatives, or even female hunters and male caregivers.

There is a famous legend in Hawaii about Pele the volcano goddess and her younger sister, Hi'iaka. In this story Pele is the unquestioned leader of a mostly female group. She has no male counterpart, no male with any authority over her, but she does have numerous lovers (not uncommon among female chiefs in Hawaiian society). One of these is Lohiau, a chief of Kauai. In the story, Pele is on the Big Island of Hawaii and wants her younger sister to go to Kauai and fetch Lohiau for her. As part of the deal, in a translation by Nathaniel Emerson, Pele says that after Hi'iaka brings Lohiau back, "…for five nights and five days he shall be mine; after that, the tabu shall be off and he shall be yours." This doesn't exactly fit the Western stereotype, but it does reflect important aspects of Hawaiian culture and the importance of cultural differences in human behavior.

My contention, then, is that most perceived differences between male and female behavior are culturally-derived. In teaching men and women around the world about relationships and how to improve them I use the same concepts and techniques for each of them, and they get the same results, because the similarities between them transcend all of the differences.

Love, Power, and Harmony

With that said, we can get on with the three primary motivators for feeling good that all human beings share. There is no need to make up any fancy names. Human beings, male and female, are all motivated either by love, or by power, or by harmony, or by various combinations of all three at the same time. Once you understand how this works, it becomes a simple thing to understand any sort of human behavior at all, including your own.

The urge to love and be loved. As a motivation, love is the urge to connect with someone or something. Humans are not very particular about what it is that they connect with, which is why we can love not only people, but places, animals, plants, things (this covers a huge range of possibilities), and ideas, plus any other category I haven't thought to mention.

In situations where fear and anger are absent, or at least weaker than the urge to connect, human beings will fall in love with each other. Cultural and personal preferences will determine whether they become lovers or just friends, but they will inevitably connect. This is the reason for the so-called "bonding" effect between individuals and within groups of any kind.

Love is part of our nature. It is the state of feeling happily connected to another, or the act of becoming connected. It is extending our self to include another. We do not have to strive for love unless we feel we do not have it. When human beings gather under circumstances where there is no fear, love simply happens. I have attended many gatherings in many different countries where dozens of complete strangers became loving friends after two or three days of just being together. What they did and why they were there didn't seem to matter. Merely close proximity and a lack of fear produced love without effort.

In times of danger love also manifests naturally. When there is a disaster or an accident, people who are not locked in fear automatically begin to assist the ones who need help. They don't have to be taught or instructed, except in how to help better. The desire to help, which is a form of love, arises spontaneously. This automatic love response is so great that some people will put their own lives at great risk to help another person, even a complete stranger. We call such people heroes when they jump into raging rivers to save someone from drowning, or run into a burning building to bring out a child, or do any one of a hundred other brave things to help another. And yet, few of these people think of themselves as heroes. Most of the time they say they did it because it was the thing to do, or they did it without thinking. It was a spontaneous act of love.

Doubt is the one thing that weakens the connection of love. When a person doubts the existence of love, then fear is born and love begins to die. Fear interferes with love because it is the opposite of love. Fear comes from feeling or being disconnected. When love diminishes, fear increases; and when fear diminishes, love increases. More than that, when love diminishes, so does the need and desire for love. Please read that last sentence again to make sure that you understand it.

The need and desire to love and be loved influence all our actions and reactions. To the degree that we feel a lack of love in any form, some form of fear will accompany that need and desire. In addition to the powerful force of sexual love, we are also driven by a love for approval and recognition. Many of our behaviors are guided by the hope of approval, or the reaction to disapproval. And many are guided by a quest for recognition, however small or temporary, especially when affection and approval do not seem imminent. Great acts that benefit all of society and vicious acts that harm society may both come from the need and desire for recognition. When recognition is lacking some people will force it by seeking respect, perhaps through doing something worthwhile, or perhaps through achieving a false respect by causing fear.

When there is sufficient frustration in satisfying the need and desire for love of any kind, the result is mental, emotional, or physical behavior that tends to disrupt relationships. This happens when the fear that results from the lack of love has no outlet. When, according to the beliefs of the individual, there is nothing that can be done, the fear causes a withdrawal inward, producing great tension in the body and therefore a greater and greater disconnection from other people.

The urge to empower and be empowered. Power is part of our nature, too. Like love, we do not have to strive for power unless we feel we do not have it. Power itself is the act of being effective. From the very moment of conception we are all in the process of expressing our power, of doing, or trying to do, that which is effective for our survival and our pleasure.

Physically, our bodies are constantly engaged in maintenance, repair, growth, learning and pleasure-seeking. Mentally, our minds are constantly engaged in problem-solving, creativity, and extending our influence into the world around us. We are always powerful, but for many reasons we may not always realize it. When the expression of power is not effective, or we do not believe that it is effective, the natural reaction is to seek a different solution to a problem or to find another way of being effective.

Inventors may experiment with thousands of different approaches before their inventions work; sports teams may try dozens of different strategies to win against their opponents; politicians may devise many different economic and social plans to achieve their ends. Individually, people try different healing techniques and approaches, different careers, different relationships, and different religions with the aim of being more effective in their lives.

Again, doubt is the one thing that weakens the natural expression of power. When a person doubts his or her personal power, or source of power, then anger is born and power begins to flee. As power decreases, anger increases; and as anger decreases, power increases. And, as with love, when power decreases, so does the need and desire for power.

The most popular technique for trying to regain power while doubt and anger are still operating is the control approach. Many people confuse power with control, but control is what people use when they are feeling powerless. Active control is used to force people to do what you want. It usually takes the form of intimidation or physical force. Passive control, also called passive aggression, takes the form of getting people to do what you want by refusing to act, or by making them feel guilty enough to do what you want. Besides being bad for relationships and effectiveness, the attempt to control causes a lot of tension in the controller.

When control isn't possible, another technique sometimes used is vandalism. A child who feels hurt and powerless may break things to display anger. This seldom works to control parents, but it does get a reaction, and that substitute for effectiveness brings a little satisfaction, at least. The child thinks, "I can't get what I want, but at least I can make someone unhappy." It is a very poor substitute for effectiveness, but it can progress from childhood tantrums to teenage vandalism to adult terrorism. And of course it brings tension with it for everyone.

However, when there is no outlet for the anger and no return to real power the anger is directed inward and the result is mental, emotional, and physical resistance to almost all other human behavior.

The urge to harmonize. Finally, there is the natural inclination toward harmony. By harmony I mean the mutually beneficial integration and cooperation of people with their social and natural environment. We can see this most easily in isolated tribal groups, but it exists also in many small communities, neighborhoods, groups, clubs and associations.

We may see attempts to create harmony by national governments and the United Nations, but the larger the group the more difficult it seems to be. This is partly because the larger the group, the easier it is for it to be more impersonal. That is, the easier it is to lose a sense of connection and personal influence. But harmony involves more than that. It really has to do with a sense of one's place and purpose in the world, and a recognition of interdependence with the rest of the world. When a person doubts that interdependence and doubts one's own place and purpose within it, then alienation is born. Instead of "you and I or we and they together" it becomes "me or us against them." Alienation, which often includes extreme confusion, restlessness, apathy, and despair, creates great internal tension and, of course, mental, emotional, and physical disharmony.

The solution for relationship problems caused by fear is to be more loving, by giving more mercy, acknowledgement, appreciation, admiration, tolerance, caring, and help to others and to yourself. The solution for relationship problems caused by anger is to increase your knowledge, skill, and self confidence. The solution for relationship problems caused by alienation is to first seek spiritual harmony with a higher or deeper being, and then look for that spirit in all things. If you want a quick fix, though, because of the ultra-fast pace of modern life, then simply cease to doubt. Keep a healthy skepticism whenever necessary, but refuse to doubt your own value, the value of others, and the value of the world. However, if that sounds too simple, keep reading.

The Rules We Live By

Many people spend their entire lives seeking to know the laws or rules of the universe, so I've decided to save them a lot of time by giving them out now, for free. Be forewarned that this is based on a shamanic view of the universe in which everything is alive, aware and responsive.

The Universe and everything in it has three aspects: Spirit, Body, and Mind. Each of these aspects has its own rules. The better we understand these rules the easier it will be for us to grow, to heal, and to have a good time.

Spirit has one rule only: "Experience existence." That's it. No conditions, no shoulds, no limits. And no avoiding it.

The Body only has two rules: "Seek pleasure" and "Avoid pain." Since the way to do this is not always clear under all circumstances, the Body will sometimes move toward pain in order to experience some associated sensory or emotional pleasure. This would be like climbing a mountain for the pleasure of the view, working out for the energy benefit, or undergoing surgery to get well. Sometimes pleasure does not seem to be an option, in which case the Body will try to move toward the least available pain. We can see this in people who drink themselves sick to suppress emotional pain, people who stay in bad relationships for fear of having none at all, and people who commit violent suicide. Then there are those who move away from pleasure for fear of an associated pain, such as people who avoid success for fear of criticism, those who believe that pleasure is a sin punishable by God, and those who believe that pleasure makes you weak. For the most part, however, it is easy to note that all spontaneous, intuitive and subconscious behavior follows the rules of seeking pleasure and avoiding pain.

What about the Mind? Hooboy! The Mind is a rule-making fanatic. It makes rules—lots and lots of rules—about everything imaginable. It makes rules about language, rules about religion, rules about behavior, even rules about the Universe. And when it wants something badly enough, why it goes ahead and changes the rules. So we have hundreds of languages around the world, hundreds of cultures based on their own ideas of right and wrong, hundreds of ways to relate to God, hundreds of scientific theories about hundreds of subjects, hundreds of countries with their own variations on political systems, hundreds of thousands of laws governing behavior in different societies... you get the idea. Ask anyone's opinion about anything and what you will hear are the rules they live by. They may call their rules opinions, beliefs or facts, but they are only rules, some inherited, some borrowed, and some made up.

Breaking rules is tricky. Just try to break the rule of Spirit. Non-existence does not seem to be an option. And when you try to break the rules of the Body you usually get severe and immediate physical or emotional consequences. The Body wants its pleasure and fears all pain, so woe to the Mind that tries to alter its natural inclinations without very good reason.

There are consequences to breaking the rules of the Mind, too, but they depend on which rules are involved and who else is involved with them. You can break a legal law with impunity if no one else is around, unless you confuse legality with morality (they do coincide, occasionally). If you break a moral law, one that you've accepted as your own, when no one else is around, you'll probably punish yourself. You can break the rules of language, but you risk being misunderstood. You can break the rules of science any time you want, as long as you are not seeking a grant, but some things may not work the way you want them to. You can break the social rules of your group, if you don't mind being cast out.

I don't recommend breaking rules. I recommend using the rules of Spirit and the Body, and playing creatively with the rules and rule-making talent of the Mind. With rules of the Mind it's much easier to make different rules than to try and break old ones. Rules that are not used any longer just fade away. You can make up any rules you want about anything you want (I'm not giving you permission; this is just something anyone can do). You can make different rules about how you think and how you feel, and what is possible, and what you can do, and about what the past means and what the future will bring. The rules you use affect your behavior and your experience. Change your rules and your life will change. This book will help you to examine the rules that you use for relationships, and to create some new ones if you want to.

What This Book Is About

This is a book about healing relationships. At the same time, this book is not about healing relationships at all.

No, I am not trying to confuse you. I am trying to help you to understand more clearly what relationships really are.

Many people today are reading, writing, teaching, and complaining about relationships. And in spite of that, too many relationships don't seem to get any better. In my counseling work I get a lot of comments like the following from clients: "My relationship just isn't working." My partner doesn't want to discuss our relationship." "I've tried everything I know to make this relationship work." "I've decided not to have another relationship." These examples could go

14

on and on, but you really don't have to read more of them because the problem is obvious.

Isn't it?

Let me make it obvious, then. The problem is that too many people spend more time on improving the relationship than they do on improving how they relate. Look at the images below:

In this first image the couple is working on their relationship. Instead of a couple, they are now a group, with the relationship as an entity practically taking on a life of its own. While I do happen to believe that everything is alive, aware, and responsive, I also know that working on "the relationship" instead of on themselves is nothing but a distraction from the real problem, because, as alive as it might be in some esoteric sense, a "relationship" is no more than an abstract, intellectual concept—a thoughtform, if you prefer—and bears no resemblance to a living, breathing, human being. Relationships don't think in any human way, they don't act, they don't change anything, they just exist like the concept "relatedness" exists, without any influence.

There is really no such thing as "a relationship" in the sense of something that exists apart from people who relate. My "relationship" with my wife is not a thing. It is merely a word for the way we relate. We can completely ignore our relationship and get along just fine. We cannot ignore the way we relate to each other and get along fine, though.

The problem between two people is never a "relationship" that isn't working. The problem is always that one or both of the people don't know how to relate to each other in a better way. That makes it a behavioral problem, not a relationship problem, and it's a lot easier to change behavior than it is to change an abstract concept called "a relationship."

In this second image the couple are relating. They are communicating, responding to each other's behavior, and creating a good relationship by the way they relate.

Is this just another book on behavior modification, then? Well, yes and no. It is a book on how to change your behavior in order to create healthier relationships with other people and the world around you, but my ideas on the best methods for doing that are a bit out of the ordinary because of my background in alternative and complementary healing.

For instance, I am going to show you how to examine physical, emotional, mental, and energetic behavior in your various relationships, and I am going to show you how to improve those relationships using objective, subjective, symbolic, and holistic techniques.

Examining Behavior

Physical behavior includes how you relate to your own body, because that influences how others will relate to you. It also includes how you move and use your body as you relate to others.

Emotional behavior has to do with your feelings about yourself and others, including how you express emotions and how you suppress them. Whether you know it or not, or even whether you believe it or not, other people can be affected subtly or dramatically by the way you feel.

Mental behavior involves everything from the words you speak to the words you think, as well as the memories, fantasies, and expectations that you dwell on. These also affect people much more than you might be aware of, and I will explain how.

Energetic behavior is based on the idea that you are more than just a bag of bones, meat and blood, and that the energy you radiate or project, consciously or subconsciously, affects other people, too.

Types of Techniques

Objective techniques include changes that you can make in your posture, your breathing, your movements, your physical actions and reactions, and your speech patterns.

Subjective techniques are based on an assumption that

telepathy is one of our natural forms of communication, and these techniques include ways of modifying your thoughts and feelings.

Symbolic techniques are based on some shamanic healing ideas involving the use of self-guided imagery to help improve relationships.

Holistic techniques include the use of role-modeling to develop patterns of behavior that might be more useful to you than the ones you've been using.

How The Book Is Organized

In order to help the greatest number of people with the greatest number of relationship problems, I have divided this book into three parts.

Part One, which includes this chapter, is about fundamental concepts and practices that affect all relationships. In addition to this chapter on relationship basics, there are chapters on criticism and praise, and on forgiveness.

Part Two is about learning how to relate better to yourself, because this is your primary relationship and the state of this one will affect all of your other relationships. First there will be a chapter on relating to your own body, then one on relating to your own mind, and then one on relating to your own spirit.

Part Three deals directly with your relationships to other people. The first chapter of this part is about relating to your family as a parent or a child or a sibling. Next is one on friends and friendship, followed by a chapter on relationships with lovers and spouses, and ending with a chapter on relationships with other people.

Every chapter will contain ideas and techniques that can be applied with a little modification to any relationships.

As many of my readers know, my teachings are based on a Hawaiian philosophy of life called Huna, which is expressed in my family tradition as a set of seven principles or ideas about life that can be applied to any endeavor or to any area of life. In keeping with that, here is a presentation of those principles as they relate to relationships:

1. The world is what you think it is, and therefore, the state, quality, or nature of a relationship is defined by you.

2. There are no limits, and you are free to change your mind about any relationship, or redefine it in any way you choose in order to change your experience of it.

3. Energy flows where attention goes, and whatever part of a relationship that you give most of your attention to is the part most energized, for good or ill.

4. Now is the moment of power, and it is in the present moment that relationships are healed, or not.

5. To love is to be happy with someone, and the more things you like about who you are relating to, the healthier and happier the relationship will be.

6. All power comes from within, and you are the one who chooses how to relate.

7. Effectiveness is the measure of truth, and if one plan for healing a relationship doesn't work, you can always make a new plan if you want to.

Now Get Ready

The music is swelling, the curtains are opening, and the great drama called "Healing Relationships" is almost ready to begin.

Eia ke kānaenae a ka mea hele: he leo, he leo wale no
This is the offering of a traveler: advice, only advice

CHAPTER TWO
CRITICISM AND PRAISE

The only way to influence someone else's behavior is to do something that motivates the person to act in the way that you want them to. I've already mentioned the motivations of love, power, and harmony. They are very effective when used properly, but the unfortunate fact is that too few people have experience in doing that. What more people do have experience in is how to use the negative motivation of fear.

One primary kind of fear that is used to motivate people is the fear of physical harm. A lot of parents use this by applying physical punishment, or the threat of it, as a means of controlling the behavior of their children. My own father had a great big leather strap, the kind that used to be found in barbershops for sharpening straight razors. He never actually had to use it on me, because simply opening the drawer he kept it was usually enough to get me to change my behavior immediately. When my behavior drove my mother into a frenzy she would whack my behind with a wooden hangar, and that motivated me for a while.

Using the fear of physical punishment as a means of motivating the behavior of people is very inefficient, however.

For one thing, the application of the punishment requires a lot of energy and attention of the part of the person meting our or supervising the punishment. For another thing, people become very adept at avoiding punishment in various ways, and even by building up a tolerance toward it. And, finally, punishment has a strong tendency to cause a great deal of suppressed anger and resentment, which can have many negative repercussions for the punishers.

Much more common, much more efficient, and much more devastating, is the act of controlling people's behavior through criticism.

The fear of criticism is probably the single greatest fear that human beings have, and, directly or indirectly, it has influenced the lives of every person on this planet. There may be some people who are free of this fear as adults, but it would be an extremely rare person who wasn't affected by it as a child. The power of using this fear as a means of control comes from the fact that everyone, innately, wants to be loved, and everyone can be trained to believe that love can be withheld. It is the threat of love being withheld that produces the fear.

Now what is the threatening thing here? It is the threat of annihilation. It is the threat of ceasing to exist, of not being nourished, of being abandoned. That's what happens when you as a young child, begin to be criticized. And what does the criticism engender? It engenders terror! Because from the point of view of a child, these people you live with, these big giants, are your support, your source of life, your source of protection, and you can't make it through life without them. And so, any threat of abandonment by them, of being turned away by them, is literally a matter of life and death. Unfortunately, as people grow older they seldom forget this early training. I worked with a woman in her sixties who had a very hard time turning down requests for help from other people, even when it had negative effects on her health and her finances. During a session involving deep focus we had the following dialogue with her subconscious.

Me: "What would happen if you said no?"

Her: "They wouldn't like me."

Me: "What would happen if they didn't like you?"

Her: "They would not want me to be around them"

Me: "And what would happen if they didn't want you to be around them?"

Her: "Then they would throw me out into the street and I would starve to death and I would die."

When she considered this dialogue with her conscious mind she knew that it came from childhood memories and was obviously absurd in the present time, but the reason why she had difficulty refusing people became clear and she was able to use this knowledge to change her behavior. The way she used the knowledge was to remind herself whenever someone asked her to do something she didn't want to do, or something that she believed was not good for her to do, that no one was going to throw her out in the street to starve and die if she said no.

The Subtle Approach To Criticism

In some families the criticism of the children is so subtle that it may not even be recognized as criticism in a conscious way by the parent or the child. In the United States in the 1950s it was still common to tell children that they were brought by a stork when they asked where they came from. Some parents jokingly tell children that they were found under a cabbage leaf, like some castaway object. Another popular comment in the States, if the parent is upset with a child's behavior, is to say that the child is going to be given back to the Indians. Parents say those things in a joking way (sometimes) and it's funny for the parents, but not to the child. It really isn't, because the subtle message to the child is that he or she doesn't really belong to the family, and this can make a small child feel tremendously insecure and unloved and somehow "wrong" for the rest of its life. After awhile the child sees the parents smile when they say such things, and the child learns to smile on the outside while his or her stomach is churning on the inside. As an adult, when accompanied by a sufficient lack of affection in the family plus a sufficient lack of self confidence and self esteem, this kind of memory can result in an inability to feel a strong connection with any group. In some cases, people may even feel alienated from the human race as a whole.

Another subtle type of criticism occurs when people think that they are encouraging someone to do better. It's a good thing to encourage someone, of course, unless there is a total lack of appreciation for accomplishment. When I was in elementary school I can remember that every time I came home with a report card, no matter how good it was, my mother would always say, "You can do better than that." She thought she was spurring me on to greater endeavors, but the effect on me was to believe that nothing I did was ever good enough, and therefore I wasn't good enough, so why try hard? It was only after ending up next to the bottom in my high school class, failing spectacularly in my first year of college, and spending three years in the U.S. Marine Corps that I got completely over that one.

A third form of subtle criticism takes place when nothing a person says or does is ever taken seriously. Often this is a kind of disempowerment technique. Older siblings may use it to keep a younger sibling subordinate, so-called friends may use it to maintain leadership control in a relationship, and parents may use it to keep children from threatening the parental hierarchy. A friend of mine told me how this played out in her house. Upon finally receiving a degree in Oriental

Medicine she went home to get some praise from her father, who immediately said, "Let's see what Uncle Jerry thinks. He had acupuncture once." This kind of criticism also tends to increase one's sense of worthlessness if it isn't counteracted.

Finally, there is the destructively insidious kind of criticism that is never spoken aloud, but is conveyed by look, gesture, or behavior. Often it is accompanied by telepathic thought, emotionally charged or not. This is not the same as a look or a gesture given by someone to let another person know that he or she has broken a rule. My wife does that when she gets a look of disapproval and flutters her hand when we are driving and she thinks I'm too close to a car in front of us. Instead, it is a look, or gesture, or movement, or thought that means "I don't like you, I don't want you, I wish you would disappear." It takes its worst form when, outwardly, the subtle critic says and does things that indicate the opposite, which leaves the victim not only confused, but unhappy and guilty for feeling that way.

The Direct Approach To Criticism

Verbal criticism that tells a person he or she has done something wrong is practically unavoidable for most people at some time or another, and while it might not be pleasant to hear, most people can handle it without serious problems, especially when it is deserved. What comes close to pure evil, in my opinion, is the constant barrage of criticism in the form of fault-finding, condemnation, blaming, disapproval, and cursing that some people inflict on others, especially when parents do it to their children. It doesn't matter if the purpose is to correct mistakes, to manipulate behavior, to vent frustration or to hide one's own feelings of inadequacy, it is a terrible thing to do to a child at whatever age. Developing self confidence and self esteem in life is hard enough without running a gauntlet of daily criticism as well. I have nothing but the highest regard for people who have survived such a critical environment to become loving, helpful, friendly human beings, and I feel deep compassion for those who are still struggling with its effects.

Direct criticism is most often used for correcting mistakes that someone has made. Although extremely popular all around the world, it is, in fact, a very inefficient method for making corrections. The problem lies in the fact that the act of criticizing produces tension in the critic as well as in the person being criticized. Too much tension interferes with memory, and that affects learning and skills. During one of my courses a woman was taking tennis lessons in her spare time. The tennis instructor used a critical approach to training until the student, using ideas from the course, instructed the instructor how to teach her by using positive reinforcement instead. Her game began to improve immediately and dramatically, which impressed the instructor quite a bit.

The Critical Effect. A baby does not learn to walk by concentrating on what it does wrong. In learning to walk it attempts a few steps, falls, gets up, tries something different, and forgets about the steps that didn't work! Encouragement and praise from parents or others for what the baby does right help the baby to learn how to walk faster. Criticism at this point would greatly inhibit the child's ability to learn how to walk. While encouragement and praise for this type of activity at this time is also extremely popular around the world, for some reason it is quickly abandoned in favor of direct criticism as a means of behavior modification once the walking is accomplished.

Between people, the use of criticism to improve a relationship is like using a hammer to heal a wound. It really doesn't work very well.

Whenever I have the opportunity during my courses and lectures I like to demonstrate the effect of criticism on the body. First I have a volunteer hold his or her hand straight out and I ask the person to hold it up strongly when I push down on it. Then I tell the person to think of a self criticism or a criticism of someone else and then I push down on his or her hand. Invariably, the person's arm becomes weaker, because his or her body has tensed up in reaction to the criticism. When I have the person think of self appreciation, or give praise to someone else, the person's arm strengthens, because the body relaxes and the person is now able to resist the pressure of my push better. The concept is similar to that employed by martial artists who are taught to keep the body relaxed until the moment of defending or striking or moving. In a variation of this demonstration I criticize the person silently and the person's arm weakens, and I praise silently and the arm strengthens.

In a relationship, there are additional effects that occur when criticism is frequent and appreciation is not. Physiologically, the frequent criticism causes an increase in physical tension in both parties, which decreases the ability to experience sensory pleasure. Emotionally, the first effect of increasing tension is to diminish the ability to feel pleasurable emotions, and the second effect is to increase sensitivity to more criticism. Because the subconscious mind has a natural tendency to move toward pleasure and away from pain, when criticism reaches the stage of feeling painful, the person being criticized will suppress emotional feelings further, causing even more tension, and will move further away from the critic either emotionally or physically or both. Meanwhile, the critic is also feeling less physical and emotional pleasure in the presence of the one being criticized. Unfortunately, this often results in more criticism to try and solve the problem.

I worked with a young couple whose marriage was in trouble because they were losing their positive feelings for each other and didn't know why. In the course of discussions with them it turned out that they had a "put down" game that they played with each other all the time that consisted of trying to outdo each other with criticisms. He would criticize her about something, then she would make a worse criticism about him, and so on. I pointed out the negative effects of criticism and the positive effects of praise, but they decided that they liked their game too much to give it up, and three months later they were divorced.

While I was in the Marine Corps two men in my unit were best friends from the same home town and they began a game called "Playing The Dozens" which was very similar to what the couple above was doing. I will never forget coming into the barracks one day to find both of them trying to kill each other after a "game" session in which one of them finally couldn't take it any more.

On the other hand, I have worked with many, many cases where couples or friends have healed failing relationships merely by dropping or reducing criticisms and greatly increasing praise and appreciation for each other.

Coping With Critics

Now let's look at the word, criticism, itself. It comes directly from the Greek word "critikos," which actually means "to discern," that is, being able to choose or see differences. But that's related to a Latin word, "discernere," which means "to separate." It is also related to the English word, "crisis." Well, when you criticize you cause a crisis, and a crisis is a turning point and the basic meaning is that there is separation. This is what is being created when there is criticism.

If it were just a case of separating things into parts so they could be looked at, that wouldn't be so bad. But criticism has been turned into a tool for emotional manipulation by creating a separation between the people being criticized and the critics. Since the separation causes unhappiness, pain, and fear, people do the best they can to cope with it.

Different people cope in different ways. Some become aggressive, some become passive, some become passive-aggressive, some of them repress all their feelings, some of them learn to cut off their emotions and become virtual walking zombies, so that they won't be hurt. Some distance themselves from others in various ways, from autism to superiority. I know that one, because I did that for a while.

I didn't become autistic. When I was a kid going into high school, I went through a stage of being "Mister Superior." Aloof. I thought I was projecting an image of cool, casual aloofness. However, at a party I turned around and there were three girls "salaaming" me behind my back, arms out and heads down as if mocking my godlike attitude. That started me looking at myself: "Hey, wait a second, this is not quite the image I thought I was projecting." It was one type of reaction I had developed to protect myself from feeling criticized that didn't work very well.

Many people develop their own of ways of protecting their feelings. Some people become pleasers. They get the idea that the way to be safe is to please everyone. A typical psychotherapeutic interpretation is that they are really trying to please their parents. In some cases that may be possible, but in most cases they developed it as a technique to cope with critical parents, and they're doing it now because it has become a habit. They have a kind of fear that someone is going to get angry with them, that someone is not going to like them. And behind that idea is that if someone doesn't like you, you've had it, you're out, out of society, cast away, abandoned to starve...

Sometimes people will not ask for favors because someone might criticize them. Some people will not ask for an extra cup of coffee in a restaurant because the waitress might get mad. Or it might inconvenience the waitress and she would give them a dirty look and they are scared to death of dirty looks, because that switches on the terror feeling of the child. They know consciously that a dirty look isn't going to hurt them, but they remember the emotional hurt of rejection and they don't know what to do about it. And so they follow the system of avoidance, avoiding situations where it might be possible that someone might criticize them, get mad at them, not like them, because those are all forms of criticism.

To further protect themselves from criticism, some people might not accept favors freely given. My mother, who was highly sensitive to criticism of any kind, direct or implied, was like that. She was a very generous woman, but she had a terrible time receiving gifts or favors. I helped her make a breakthrough of sorts when I asked her if doing things for other people gave her pleasure. When she told me it did, I asked her if she loved her children. When she said that of course she did, I asked her why she was denying her children the pleasure of doing things for her. She was a lot easier to do favors for after that.

Some people make up criticism because they've been trained as a child to expect it, no matter what they do. They are so bound up with the idea that something's wrong with them, so fearful of it, that someone will say something and they'll make up a criticism out of it. For instance, I was talking with someone who was a dancer, and I said, "You're a dancer. That's very interesting. You know I saw this dance group last night and there was this one person who was really outstanding, really enjoying it..." And here I was sharing this experience because I thought she would be interested, and she was saying to herself, "He thinks she's a better dancer than I am. There's something wrong with me. He's really putting me down, and I resent that." You can't even talk to these kinds of people sometimes about anyone else because they'll think it's a put-down on them. What a sad way to live. And how terrible that feels, because whenever someone talks about someone else, this kind of person feels awful because they always compare themselves in a negative way with the person being discussed, no matter what the discussion is about.

This fear of criticism from other people is so pervasive it's scary, especially if you start looking at all the things you do in your life based on what other people might say or do. I asked a woman friend about this and she thought a bit, then said that she would estimate that ninety-percent of her waking life was devoted to worrying about what other people might think about her behavior.

As an adult I thought I had rid myself of that kind of fear that I had learned as a child. Well, I was attending a conference with my wife not long ago, and during a break in the three-hour lecture someone got up in front to take us through a kind of aerobic exercise that we could do right there standing up by our chairs. It was really a great way to get your limbs moving and your muscles limber. So we're standing there and the instructor says, "Raise your arms and wiggle your bottom" and I felt this feeling of embarrassment. It's like this little voice inside was saying, "You're not going to move like that. What would people think? What would people say if they see you moving like that? You'll look foolish, you'll look silly." And it was amazing to me to hear this voice going on inside me, and I said, "Hey! Self! Everybody here is doing it! Look around! Nobody's sitting down at all. Everybody's waving their hands and twitching their bottom around. Who's going to say something?"

I realized in examining my reaction later that it was a habit response. It didn't have anything to do with somebody actually standing there ready to say, "You're foolish." It had to do with a habit of not wanting to look foolish in general. And since I don't usually run around with my arms waving and wiggling my bottom in that kind of a setting, a habit response came up of "Ooh/ah, terrible, don't! They'll throw you out, abandon you, you'll starve to death," and that whole sequence that was learned in childhood goes on. Once I was able to see that and let myself know it was okay to act in a weird way, I had no problem and joined in and did it with the best of them. But I had to deal with it first. I had to consciously let myself know that there was no danger.

Here are some useful ways to cope with critics.

Critical awareness. Often we don't even notice how critical we and the others around us are.

1. Go on a critical diet for seven days. For one full week, do your best not to criticize anyone or anything, aloud or mentally. That includes you, too.

2. When someone does something wrong, tell them what to do right if you have to say something, but don't criticize. If something goes wrong, fix it if you can, but don't criticize it.

3. Pay attention to how much others around you criticize people or things or situations, but don't criticize them for it.

4. Notice how you feel when you try not to criticize. Pleased? Anxious? Helpless? Angry? Your reactions may help you to discover the motivations behind your criticisms.

5. If you can go a full seven days without criticizing the first time you try it, you are exceptional.

Coping with embarrassment. Here's a way to turn what I said above about this subject into a technique.

1. Think about a situation in which you either felt embarrassed or imagine that you might feel embarrassed.

2. Give yourself permission to act the way you did or the way you might act, regardless of what people think.

3. Tell yourself that you won't be abandoned, you won't be cast out, and you won't starve to death because of it.

4. Repeat this until you can remember the incident, or imagine an incident, without feeling embarrassed.

Every time you act out of fear you reinforce the fear. Every time you do something to avoid criticism, you increase the fear of criticism until it's running your life. And if that's what's running your life, you are not a free person. You are no longer doing things out of choice. You're doing things because "The Masters" all around you are telling you what to do. It's time to get your freedom back. No one has the right to be your judge (unless you do something illegal). Not your parents, not anyone else. No one has that right, although a lot of people will try and assume it because, subconsciously or not, they are trying to be your parent.

Coping with substitute parents. These are the people who tell you how to speak, how to stand, how to sit, how to act, how to dress, and how to feel, without being paid for it. They may be disguised as relatives, friends or teachers, but they are acting like critical parents. This next technique is based on logical reinterpretation, and it works because your subconscious is very logical, once you give it an acceptable assumption.

1. Recall a time when you were being criticized by a parent. There may be many such incidents and if so, apply what follows to each of them, one at a time.

2. For each incident, tell yourself strongly, "That wasn't criticism, that was an opinion. That did not mean that anything was wrong with me, or that I was bad. An opinion was being expressed about my behavior and that's all. So what?" Repeat this until you feel differently about the incident.

3. Apply this to any "substitute parents" in your life.

The effect of this will be to take away the power of the statements said about you, and when they are no longer powerful they are no longer dangerous, and you no longer have the same reactions.

Coping with critical memories. This one deals directly with your feelings about a memory of being criticized. It works very well for most people most of the time, but not so well for severely traumatic incidents.

1. Recall a time when you were criticized.

2. Imagine antlers growing out of the head of the person criticizing you.

3. Imagine that person dressed in a clown costume while a band plays circus music behind him or her.

4. Add anything else you want to make the situation as silly and ridiculous as possible, and notice how your feelings about the incident have changed.

Coping with critical memories – variation.

1. Recall a time when you were being criticized.

2. Freeze the memory into a sheet of ice or turn it into a sheet of glass.

3. Imagine a hammer in your hand and break up the ice or glass into little pieces.

4. If it's ice, let it melt and evaporate away. If it's glass, put it in a trash can and have someone take it to the dump. Notice how your feelings have changed.

And that's how you cope with critics, whether they come from outside or inside.

How To Criticize

What do you do if someone does something wrong and the only way you know how to correct the situation is to criticize the person? Well, if you absolutely must criticize, then you may as well do it in the most effective way possible.

The Open Face Sandwich Technique. This works well

because people are more open to receiving criticism when their accomplishments are acknowledged.

1. Make the criticism without anger, and with a clear indication of how you want it to be corrected.

2. Compliment the person on something else, no matter how small or even apparently insignificant, that was accomplished in a good manner.

The concept behind this is very simple. Remember the criticism experiment I described further back. Criticism causes tension and praise relaxes. A person who receives praise for an accomplishment is much more likely to listen to a criticism and do something to correct it. The key, though, is to criticize first and praise second. I know that this goes against the more typical pattern of praising first if you praise at all, and ending with the criticism, but physiologically and psychologically the pattern I that I describe here has much better effects.

One of the best examples of this that I know of happened when my wife was the consultant for the dietary departments of a large chain of hospitals. Part of her job was to make reports to the State of California on the condition of the kitchens. On her first visit to a hospital that her corporation had just acquired she found the kitchen in a deplorable condition, and employee morale was very low.

It was common for a person in her position to fill the report with everything that was wrong, without paying any attention to what might be right. In fact, noting anything good was uncommon in her profession. My wife, however, knew the effects of praise, so she searched the kitchen high and low for anything that had been done right. She finally found a faucet that was clean and bright and noted this one good thing prominently in her report. The kitchen staff was pleasantly shocked to find that something good had been acknowledged, and that was the beginning of a turnaround for the kitchen operation and for employee morale.

The Closed Face Sandwich Technique. Very similar to the above, and even more effective. It does take a little more effort and sometimes creativity to apply, though.

1. Give a compliment.
2. Give a criticism.
3. Give a compliment.

People who encounter these two techniques for the first time are often afraid that giving compliments along with criticism will diminish the force or the importance of the criticism, when in fact the opposite is what happens. If the critic consciously or unconsciously uses criticism as a control technique, he or she may find it harder to apply the Sandwiches effectively.

The Power Of Praise

The words "praise" and "compliment" are so similar in English that they are used interchangeably, although "praise" has a somewhat stronger and more personal connotation. You can compliment a woman on her hairdo or a man on his watch, but you wouldn't usually say you were praising them. Nevertheless, I will use whichever word that I feel is suitable for the sentence.

Praise is definitely powerful, because it makes you feel good. More accurately, I ought to say that it makes your body feel good. Your mind is another matter. Your body will always feel good when you receive praise, unless you have personal or cultural rules which say that receiving verbal praise is bad or socially unacceptable. In that case you may feel embarrassed or worse when someone openly gives you a compliment. Silent or telepathic compliments that bypass your conscious mind will always make your body feel good. The same holds true when you praise or compliment other people. When someone you know has difficulty accepting praise or compliments, just do it silently. Their body will accept it happily and their mind won't interfere.

A silent praise experience. Try this on yourself to feel the effects of this practice.

> 1. Mentally compliment your entire body from the top of your head all the way through to the bottom of your feet, including skin, bones, organs, and everything you can think of. An easy way to do this is to say something like, "Thank you skin for covering my body, thank you brain for thinking, thank you heart for pumping my blood, etc."
>
> 2. When you've finished with your body, compliment your less tangible attributes like skills and talents, imagination and memory.
>
> 3. Notice how your body reacts and whether you feel calm or excited or pleased.

The power of praise is due to the fact that it makes you feel connected to those giving the praise, even when it is you doing it to yourself, and it is this sense of connection that feels so good and that releases tension, which in turn feels good, too. The sense of connection may also be interpreted by various people as being loved, admired, appreciated, acknowledged, recognized, etc.

Since people tend to move toward pleasure and away from pain, praise is a good motivator except when it is insincere. In most cases, your body can feel when praise is insincere, and then it does not have the same physiological response. Some people, however, including some actors, performers, and dictators, are so desperate for any kind of connection that they will accept all sorts of insincere or even forced praise.

As powerful as praise is, and as good as it feels, a surprising number of people don't know how to do it. Here are some excerpts from a booklet on blessing that I wrote called *The Little Pink Booklet of Aloha*. In this booklet, and elsewhere, I equate blessing with compliments and praise:

Blessing may be done with imagery or touch, but the most usual and easy way to do it is with words. The main kinds of verbal blessing are:

Admiration - This is the giving of compliments or praise to something good that you notice. E.g., "What a beautiful sunset; I like that flower; you're such a wonderful person."

Affirmation - This is a specific statement of blessing for increase or endurance. E.g., "I bless the beauty of this tree; blessed be the health of your body."

Appreciation - This is an expression of gratitude that something good exists or has happened. E.g., "Thank you for helping me; I give thanks to the rain for nourishing the land."

Anticipation - This is blessing for the future. E.g., "We're going to have a great picnic; I bless your increased income; Thank you for my perfect mate; I wish you a happy journey; May the wind be always at your back."

In order to gain the most benefit from blessing, you will have to give up or cut way down on the one thing that negates it: cursing. This doesn't mean swearing or saying "bad" words. It refers to the opposite of blessing, namely criticizing instead of admiring; doubting instead of affirming; blaming instead of appreciating; and worrying instead of anticipating with trust. Whenever any of these are done they tend to cancel out some of the effects of blessing. So the more you curse the harder it will be and the longer it will take to get the good from a blessing. On the other hand, the more you bless the less harm any cursing will do.

Here, then, are some ideas for blessing various needs and desires. Apply them as often as you like, as much as you want to get the best effects.

Health - Bless healthy people, animals, and even plants; everything which is well made or well constructed; and everything that expresses abundant energy.

Happiness - Bless all that is good, or the good that is in all people and all things; all the signs of happiness that you see, hear or feel in people or animals; and all potentials for happiness that you notice around you.

Prosperity - Bless all the signs of prosperity in your environment, including everything that money helped to make or do; all the money that you have in any form; and all the money that circulates in the world.

Success - Bless all signs of achievement and completion (such as buildings, bridges, and sports events); all arrivals at destinations (of ships, planes, trains, cars and people); all signs of forward movement or persistence; and all signs of enjoyment or fun.

Confidence - Bless all signs of confidence in people and animals; all signs of strength in people, animals and objects (including steel and concrete); all signs of stability (like mountains and tall trees); and all signs of purposeful power (including big machines, power lines).

Love and Friendship - Bless all signs of caring and nurturing, compassion and support; all harmonious relationships in nature and architecture; everything that is connected to or gently touching something else; all signs of cooperation, as in games or work; and all signs of laughter and fun.

Inner Peace - Bless all signs of quietness, calmness, tranquility, and serenity (such as quiet water or still air); all distant views (horizons, stars, the moon); all signs of beauty of sight, sound or touch; clear colors and shapes; the details of natural or made objects.

Spiritual Growth - Bless all signs of growth, development and change in Nature; the transitions of dawn and twilight; the movement of sun, moon, planets and stars; the flight of birds in the sky; and the movement of wind and sea.

The previous ideas are for guidance if you are not used to blessing, but don't be limited by them. Remember that any quality, characteristic or condition can be blessed (e.g., you can bless slender poles and slim animals to encourage weight loss), whether it has existed, presently exists, or exists so far in your imagination alone.

Personally I have used the power of blessing to heal my body, increase my income, develop many skills, create a deeply loving relationship with my wife and children, and to establish a worldwide network of peacemakers working with the aloha spirit. It's because it has worked so well for me that I want to share it with you. Please share it with as many others as you can.

CHAPTER THREE
THE ART OF FORGIVENESS

Forgiveness is one of the most beautiful experiences you can have. You might not think about it that way right now, but I hope you will by the end of this chapter. Forgiveness is not only beautiful in itself for the feeling that arises in you when you forgive someone or something, but it is beautiful because of the greater results that come from doing it.

The word for forgiveness in Hawaiian is *kala*, and it contains a lot of very interesting meanings. One of the most important is the meaning of release, because that's the essence of forgiveness. A common misconception about forgiveness is that it is something you do for the person who did something wrong. While that person may benefit from your forgiveness, especially if he or she is in danger of being punished if you don't forgive, the main beneficiary is the person who forgives, because true forgiving releases all the anger tension that you may have about something.

The act of forgiving can release tension energy that you've blocked and held back within yourself because you've been trying to hold it against someone, including yourself.

If you can release that, it gives you tremendous energy that can be put into the direction or path that you want to go. Included in that is the full awakening of all your inner powers and the increase of happiness beyond anything you ever dreamed possible.

Some people would think that's an outrageous statement, but all you have to do is to remember that excessive physical tension interferes with the functioning of body, mind, and spirit, and that is why it inhibits your access to happiness and your inner powers. And all you have to add to that for the moment is the fact that anger, guilt and resentment all cause excessive tension.

What is true forgiveness? First, I will tell you what it is not. It is not simply saying the words, "I forgive you." That is only a formal way of acknowledging forgiveness, and is not the act of forgiveness itself. Forgiveness can be done without any words at all.

Technically speaking, forgiveness is the act of deciding not to punish someone, or wish punishment for someone, for something he or she did. Realistically, forgiveness is the state in which you no longer feel angry about what the person did. It is also the process by which you reach that state. There are many ways to forgive someone, and many techniques that can be applied, but forgiveness only happens when a particular process occurs.

The Forgiveness Process. Here's what happens.

1. Someone (maybe even you) does something that breaks one of your serious rules.

2. You get angry (this may take different forms, such as simple anger, rage, jealousy, envy, resentment, feelings of betrayal, guilt, etc.).

3. You want the person to be punished in some way (physically, emotionally, mentally).

4. For some reason or another, and by some means or

another, you change your mind about how you feel about the person and/or about the event.

Why is it so hard to forgive? This is a very important point to understand. The difficulty in forgiving someone is usually based on the ideas you have about forgiveness. Here are some common ideas that make forgiveness difficult:

1. You believe that what the person did was unforgivable and you refuse to change your mind about that.

2. You believe that by forgiving you are doing the person a favor, and you really don't want to do that.

3. You believe that forgiving means forgetting and you are afraid that if you forget the incident you will allow the same thing or similar things to happen to you again.

Let's look at these three ideas in turn.

Forgiving the Unforgivable. You have the right to keep any rules about right and wrong, good and bad that you have. Likewise, you have the right never to forgive someone, including yourself, for something that was done, or not done. The problem is not with being unforgiving. The problem is with the consequences of that, for as long as you remain unforgiving your levels of inner tension will keep increasing, year by year, with increasingly serious physical, emotional, and mental effects. It would seem at first glance that the only possibilities would be to pay the price of not forgiving, or pay the same price—ever-increasing tension—by betraying your deepest values.

I'm mainly talking about the kind of tension energy that's built up from hate. The word, "hate," scares some people, but a euphemism like "intense dislike," just doesn't carry the same feeling. It is ongoing hate that makes something seem unforgivable. Some people are pretty tough, because they can handle chronic hate for quite a few years, until eventually the body begins to break down. Some people are more sensitive and begin to experience the negative effects of hate

42

tension almost immediately. There are many different factors involved in this, but forgiveness is the one factor that can release it.

It doesn't matter how old you are. I know people in their seventies who still hate their parents, and that will interfere with their happiness even at that age. Somehow or other they have to release the stranglehold that the parental image still has on them. Their parents might be gone physically, but as long as they are still there in a person's mind, and there is still hate for what they did or didn't do, they still control the person's life.

Using parents as an example, here are some things that might be helpful. Realize first of all, that your parents weren't God. They weren't intended to be. They were just normal human beings with their own fears and their own misunderstandings, their own attempts to do things, however they may have botched it up, but they were doing the best they could. Even though that may not have been very good, it was the best they could do, based on who they were and what they believed. If you can acknowledge this, that's a step forward, because now you may be able to forgive them for being so ignorant. Or forgive them for not knowing how to love you better. Or maybe you can simply forgive them for being dumb. Forgive them, and that means "I release you from any desire for punishment, for having been so dumb."

You don't release them for having hurt you. You don't have to do that. But if you can release them for anything, then you can realize that everything else was just a consequence of their stupidity, or their ignorance, or not knowing how to act different, or for just being mean people by nature, or whatever else it might have been. If you have really nice parents and you've never had any problem with them, you can put this one aside. This is for those of you who have had some real difficulties with people that you have to deal with.

So if you can forgive such people, whether parents or others, for some aspect of their behavior or beliefs, like not knowing how to be a better parent, for trying too hard, for not being strong, for things over which they may not have had any control, then that will tend to release the pressure on you, the tension between you and them, or between you and your memories of them. And more of your energy will begin to be released for your own health and happiness.

Of course, it's very easy to tell someone to forgive, and I know that carrying it out is not that easy. So I'm not just saying to forgive someone you hate, I'm going to tell you how. There have to be ways and means to put these ideas into practice or it would be useless for me to talk about doing it.

Forgiving the forgivable. There is a solution to this, an unusual solution, admittedly. I know, because I have used it. In my life I have encountered people who did terrible things, either to me or to those I love and yet, by forgiving in a particular way, I can still think that what they did was terrible without having any tension about it. What I did may not work for everyone, but in case it can work for someone, here it is:

> 1. Acknowledge that what the person did was wrong, very wrong, that it always was wrong and always will be wrong.
>
> 2. At the same time, forgive the person for being the kind of person who would not or could not have acted any differently. Or, if it's appropriate, forgive the person for not being able, or not knowing how, to have acted any differently.
>
> 3. Repeat this, changing the wording as necessary, until you can remember the incident without feeling any anger or tension.

The key to making this work for you is to put your focus on forgiving the forgivable. Instead of trying to forgive a terrible deed, you forgive the fact that the person had a flawed character. To the degree that you can think differently about any aspect of the person or the incident in a way that relieves your feeling about it, you will be free of that much tension in regard to it.

Forgiving As A Favor. The more powerless a person feels, the more likely he or she is to think that forgiving someone is the same as giving them the power to act the same way again. This is not the case at all.

Forgiving is an internal act that affects you more than anyone else. And the greatest effect it has on you is to increase your own power, or give it back to yourself. It confers no benefit to the other person unless, as I mentioned above, it helps them to avoid punishment, or if they care how you feel. However, a person who deserves punishment can still be punished even though you have forgiven them in your heart.

Let's say for instance that someone did something to you that involved a lawsuit. You can forgive that person, and still follow through with the lawsuit, because you are pursuing your rights under the law. What matters in terms of your emotional and mental health is the spirit in which you do it. If you pursue the lawsuit in a spirit of revenge, the whole thing will backfire on you. But if you go at it with a common sense acknowledgment of asserting your rights to whatever rights or damages you have in this situation, then it's going to be much easier and you're going to be much more successful if you have a good cause. So the major thing is not what you're doing, but the spirit in which you are doing it.

Yes, there is a fine line between seeking justice and seeking revenge, but it's a vital line in terms of your happiness and your effectiveness. If you're going into something like that and you really want to be effective, you must be clear about what your goals are. If your goals are to redress a grievance, to make things as right as they can be again, to get some justice in your terms in a particular case, that's worthy and honorable. Most legal systems are set up for that. But if you are only out to hurt the other person, to punish them, to make them cry for mercy, or something like that, as much as you might feel it's justified, it isn't really effective for you in the long term if you keep maintaining negative feelings.

When you are feeling emotions of resentment toward your parents, toward a lover of some kind, toward a friend or whatever, or even toward the world in general, it's because you're constantly dwelling on what that other person did to you or didn't do for you. That makes you angry. And the more you dwell on that, the more blocked energy you build up. And it doesn't have to happen.

There is an aspect of this, however, that needs to be addressed. Revenge has a very seductive quality about it that makes it hard to resist for some people. In the United States popular ideas are often stated on bumper stickers, and one that was very popular for a while was "Don't get mad, get even." I never understood why people would be so drawn to that until I was working with one of my sons who was talking about getting revenge on one of his friends and I said, "Now tell me, would that really make you feel good to do that?" He said, "Yeah!" So I had to sit and think about that and review it, and talk to him some more, and I realized he was right, there really would be a temporary good feeling from doing that. No doubt about it. And the temporary good feeling comes from the sense of somehow being effective in that moment. You have felt helpless, you felt out of control, and getting even is a way of feeling back in control again.

But I say it's a false sense of power, because the only thing it's effective for is giving you that temporary jolt of good feeling, like a drug. As far as changing situations goes, it's not very effective, because the problem will just come back again, either from that person or someone else. That kind of energy goes out and that kind of energy has to come back, usually in the form of a backlash of revenge, a lifelong vendetta, or a feud that lasts for centuries. It is not what I would call an effective technique for changing your feelings. There are better ways to be assertive, to do what you feel is clearly right, and yet not use the energy of destruction or destroying to do it.

Some people actually believe that by not forgiving they are punishing the other person. And they may believe that withholding forgiveness gives them a sort of power over the other person. In this case, forgiveness, or the lack of it, is being used to manipulate the other person. Although the person withholding forgiveness still has to deal with the tension, the person who is not being forgiven may react with fear or emotional hurt if they care enough about how the manipulator feels. However, those victims of such manipulation who are reading this need not be affected much longer, because later on I will tell them how to get free of this trap.

In forgiving people, remember that you are not making what they did right. You are not saying that what they did was good. You're releasing them because your feelings of anger or resentment have been holding you back in the present moment. You're releasing the energy that's keeping you sometimes poor, sometimes unsuccessful, sometimes unhealthy, sometimes without a good relationship, and that's all you're doing. What you're doing now, today, what you're intending to do tomorrow, is so much more important than anything that happened in the past.

The powerful idea that I want to share with you now is to give permission to someone else to be the way they are, and to do what they do. Or to be the way they were and to do what they did. That act of giving permission for them to be that way is an act of forgiveness. And the effect that can suddenly come from this is miraculous. It can also release all the problems of disappointment, because how can you be disappointed with someone if you've already given them permission to be what they are and to do what they do? Then whatever they do, while you may not like it and you may have a few moments of disillusionment or even of disappointment, the feeling doesn't last long if you remember, "Wait a second! I gave them permission to be what they are and to do what they do, and so whatever they do, even though I don't like it, I don't have to stay disappointed."

This is because disappointment comes from not forgiving, and resentment comes from disappointment. Think about what disappointment really means. It is no more than the feeling that comes when things didn't turn out the way you wanted. You had it in mind that something was going to be a certain way, and it wasn't that way, and so you feel angry or resentful about it. It is understandable to feel like this for a few moments, but why carry it on? And why let that limit you from moving forward in the future? Because you're afraid you might be disappointed again? I've met an amazing number of people who avoid potentially happy relationships because they might be disappointed. That doesn't make a whole lot of sense, since disappointment comes from a choice about deciding to feel bad when something happens that you don't like. For those who want to be able to forgive without fear, I will now present a technique that will help you to forgive and to feel more powerful at the same time. Oddly enough, it seems like you are doing the other person a favor, but it is really you who are the beneficiary.

Giving Permission.

1. Think of a person whom you've decided to forgive, but are afraid to or don't know how.

2. Imagine that you are the Rulemaker of the Universe and, out of the generosity of your heart, give that person permission to be what he or she is and to

do what he or she does, or to be what he or she was, and to have done what he or she did.

3. From now on, whenever you think of what happened, remind yourself that you gave permission. The effect of this, over time, is to diminish any fear you may have had and to transfer to power of the happening to you, as far as feeling goes.

Forgiving And Forgetting. The reason I say it this way is that forgiving is not the same as forgetting. The idea behind the admonition to "forgive and forget" is misunderstood. The real basis for it is the fact that when you truly forgive something it may become so unimportant that you forget about it. Unfortunately, when forgiveness is needed, many people try to forget by suppressing or pushing down the memory of what happened out of their consciousness and refuse to think about it. While it may be good not to dwell on the incident that needs forgiving, the problem is that by pushing it into the background without any resolution they are still dwelling on it. It's constantly there in the subconscious awareness and it keeps trying to surface so they can do something about it, but they keep shoving it aside and pretending it's not there, even though they know it is, with the result that no forgiveness is taking place. And forgetting is not happening, either.

Sometimes forgetting about the memory completely, even if you do forgive, can work in your worst interests. If you forgive someone for harming you in some way, and then you actually forget it, or suppress it so well you can't remember it, you may find yourself in the same situation with the same person again. If a man or woman has swindled you out of half your life's savings and you decide to forgive and forget, then that person has a good chance of swindling you out of the other half of your life's savings. I have a number of friends who have done moderate harm to myself and to my organization. They are still my friends because I have

49

forgiven them, and because I remember what happened and take care not to let such opportunities for harm occur again. I give permission to my friends to make mistakes so that we can still be friends. But I do my best to make sure that the same mistakes won't be made again, at least around me. That way I can keep my friends and enjoy those aspects of our friendship that still work.

On the other hand, pretending to forget can actually lead to a healing in some cases. During my work in Senegal, West Africa, I established a reputation in the diplomatic and business communities for my negotiating skills. It happened that an American company had made a contract with the Senegalese government to drill for wells in a particular province. However, no one had notified the quasi-autonomous military governor of that province, so he promptly jailed all the Americans on site and confiscated their equipment. Negotiations between the governor, the American Embassy, and the central government of Senegal made no headway because the governor would not forgive the slight to his authority. That's when I was asked to help.

First, I made an appointment to see the governor, without specifying the purpose. Then I met with the president of the American company told him to let me do all the talking, and to trust me no matter what I said. Next, the company president and I went to see the governor.

To the company president the whole event seemed surreal. I greeted the governor, whom I already knew, and introduced the company president. I told the governor that his company was interested in helping the governor to find more water for the agricultural activities of his province. The governor said he thought that sounded like a good idea. Finally, the governor and I set a date for the beginning of the American project. At no time was the existing situation mentioned, although we both knew what it was, and we both knew we knew. While we were talking, the American workers were in jail, and the American equipment was sitting in a provincial warehouse. The governor and I, however, both pretended nothing had happened, which allowed us to negotiate without any history to deal with.

After the meeting, the company president was furious with me for not dealing with what he thought was the problem, which was that of his men and his equipment. I told him that the real problem was the affront to the governor's authority, that we had dealt with that, and that the other problems would be resolved as a result. His trust in me was shaky at that point, but two weeks later he accompanied me to the drilling site and there were his men and his equipment, all set up and ready to go.

By maintaining an awareness of the unpleasant event, and by not bringing it up, we were able to start over without rancor or criticism or blame. The effect of this was to desensitize the event, to take away its emotional charge, and this gave all of us the freedom to move forward. The same approach may work for you sometimes in your relations with friends, as long as those friends value the friendship more than their need to be in the right.

As I mentioned above, the more unimportant an event becomes, the easier it is to forget it in a natural way. As a technique for forgiveness, then, the emphasis is on disempowering the event, rather than on forgetting it.

Time-shift Forgiveness. This technique works well as a means of forgiving—changing your mind and feelings about—an event or a person that is no longer part of your current life.

> 1. Think about the event that you want to forgive. Then be aware of your current situation.
> 2. Remind yourself that that was then and this is now, and that what happened then is no longer important

51

now because it no longer exists now.

3. Repeat this every time the event comes to mind.

Partial Forgiveness. Sometimes a relationship problem seems so big that the idea of forgiving is too overwhelming. In that case, you can start off by forgiving a little bit and work your way up to more. There's no cosmic law that says you have to forgive everything all at once. You can do it in bits and pieces, a little bit at a time, as long as you get started with it.

I can recall one woman I worked with who had a very difficult time forgiving her husband for something. She had a tremendous amount of tension that was producing some severe physical problems, but she still didn't feel she could forgive him. So we kind of negotiated for a while, and what we came up with was that she figured that at least she could send a ball of love or forgiveness, a little pink ball about one inch in diameter, for one second. She could do that much. I'd have negotiated down to a nanosecond if necessary, and have it be a millimeter in diameter, just to get her to do something. Anyway, she figured she could send a one-inch ball of love for one second. That much she could handle. Well, you know, that was a hundred percent more than she was doing before, because she was doing nothing before. What happened after several weeks of continually sending that one-inch ball of pink light was that she gradually became able to send a six-foot ball of light for one whole minute! The result of this was that her body was beginning to loosen up, and she was feeling more free of the aches and pains and insecurities and stuff that she had been feeling before, that she'd been causing herself by her attitude toward her husband. Try this:

1. Think of a person you want to forgive, but can't seem to do it completely.

2. Make a decision to forgive that person just a tiny bit for a small amount of time, like one second.

52

3. Imagine a symbol for that forgiveness that appeals to you. It could be a one-inch or one-centimeter ball of pink light, a single note of music, or anything else that suits you.

4. Imagine sending or giving this small bit of forgiveness to the person in question.

5. Continue doing this on a regular basis, gradually increasing the time or the size or the notes or whatever as you are able until the forgiveness feels as complete as it can be.

Self Forgiveness. Self forgiveness is needed when you have a problem with guilt. Guilt is created when you believe you have done something wrong, or when you feel that something about you is wrong. The latter leads to feelings of inadequacy, and then to feelings of guilt because you don't know what to do about it.

If it's a question of having done something wrong, then you can either correct the wrong if that's possible, or use some of the techniques given above to forgive yourself. If it's a question of feeling guilty because you feel inadequate in some way, then that requires a different approach.

Often, the parents create a sense of inadequacy in the child when the child is made responsible for the parents' happiness. The same thing may happen with other family members, other authority figures, and even friends, lovers, or spouses. The concept puts the person into an impossible position, because he or she has no control over another person's feelings or decisions. When this kind of thing happens, the basic message received by the person is, "You are responsible for my happiness, so if I'm not happy there's something wrong with you and you can't have my love."

In undertaking the impossible task of pleasing the parents or anyone else in order to survive and to be loved, many people grow up feeling really inadequate, feeling that something's wrong with them. Because that's such a devastating idea, sometimes they react by trying to cover up the inadequacy with anger turned back on the parents or toward other people, but underlying all of it is that sense of personal inadequacy. If they can find that sense of personal adequacy, that sense of being loved and loveable, then that can give them a sense of power, the power to fulfill their dreams, to do and be what they want to do and be. But, where is that going to come from?

Many people search the world for someone else to give them support, for someone to love them, while they're not doing the same thing for themselves. Well folks, I hate to disappoint you out there if you are one of them, but it just isn't going to happen. Life doesn't work that way. You will find some real masters of living in the world who can love you in spite of yourself, but for the most part you will simply find people who will react to you the way you react to yourself. And if you have that sense of something being wrong with you, you are broadcasting that out both subtly through your behavior and telepathically, and other people will tend to respond to your own way of thinking about yourself by thinking about you that way, too.

The healing of this relationship with yourself begins with self loving, and this is what leads to self forgiveness. And self loving means making yourself responsible for your own happiness by learning how to love yourself.

It can begin with as simple a thing as telling yourself "I love you," no matter how you actually feel about that right now. You can talk to your body first, and tell your body—your head, your hands, your feet, your skin, your bones, your hair, your organs, and all the rest of it—"I like you, I love you, you're pretty nice." Even if at first you don't quite mean it and even if at first it might feel a little silly, so what? The rewards of silliness sometimes are very well, worth it. And if you start that process, then you might talk to your mind and tell it the same thing, and you might talk to your soul and your spirit and your energy and whatever it takes, to yourself as a whole, somehow start telling yourself, "Hey, I like you, I think you're pretty nice, I think you're okay, no matter what happened, no matter what you've done, I love you."

I can already hear a lot of objections from people, and the loudest one is, "How can I love myself if I know I don't deserve it?" The short answer is, "Just do it anyway." The long answer is, "You have to practice unconditional love." That is such an important aspect of forgiveness, and especially self forgiveness, that I have to discuss it more in depth.

Unconditional Love. If we were to search for the "highest," most consistent, cross-cultural, ethical, philosophical and spiritual guideline for living, it would probably be "to love one another." Not only is this idea found all over the Earth, but according to many sources even aliens are telling us to do it.

It's an easy thing to say, and it feels like the right thing to do, but how do we really love one another in a world of lies, deceit, murder, abuse, torture, ignorance, and people who are simply exasperatingly irritating? How do we get from the words to the act without just acting a part and being false to our real feelings?

Actually, we could start out by acting a part with pretty good effect. Pretending to love each other is a lot better than killing each other, after all, and we can see this approach in practice at diplomatic functions, whenever a losing team cheers the winning one, and when beauty contest runner-ups congratulate the new queen. If we are observant, we can see it in a lot of personal relationships as well. However, the problem with this solution is that it is extremely stressful, both for the pretender and the pretendee, and especially in long-term relationships. Our subconscious is very aware of

55

the feelings within us and around us, even when our conscious mind denies them. There has to be a better way.

There is another solution offered by some. It's called "unconditional love." The idea is to remove all judgments in your thinking and feeling of good and bad, right and wrong, pleasurable and painful, etc. Then, so the teaching goes, you'll be able to love everyone and everything equally, under all conditions and in all situations.

Unfortunately, this is not really a solution; it's an idealization. A solution to a problem implies a manner or method or plan for achieving a resolution. Proposing unconditional love as a solution to human relationships is like saying, "If only people would stop fighting we could all live in peace." Yeah, right, so how do we do that? How do you get from conditional love to unconditional love? If the only method is years and years of meditative exercises, then this is not a viable solution, either for the majority of individuals living their daily lives, or for society as a whole.

Another difficulty with the concept of unconditional love, nice as it sounds, is that it's unconditional. Think about it: no conditions at all. No rules or laws for human behavior; no incentive for healing or caring, or creativity and invention; no reason for loving any one person more than another, no matter how they look or act; no desire for learning or teaching or challenge. Because all of these things require judgment of some kind. The end result of unconditional love would be like living in the Garden of Eden again. Some people think that would be great; some think that getting kicked out of the nest was the best thing that ever happened to Adam and Eve, hard as it's been.

Finally, let's put unconditional love to rest with a very practical consideration. Any solution to the problem of how to love one another has to be progressive. In other words, it has to start somewhere and grow. Regardless of what you think about it, for unconditional love to work in a wide-spread way it would require some sort of magical, instant transformation of everyone at the same time. Otherwise, all those conditional people would make life extremely difficult and dangerous for their lovers and friends and neighbors who were trying to be unconditional. On the other hand, the latter probably wouldn't even notice, if they survived. This is probably why those who practice unconditional love usually start out in caves and on mountaintops, far from where most people live.

As a proponent of creative conditional love, I believe that we can learn to love each other to a far greater degree than we do. This approach is conditional because it recognizes the usefulness of having comparisons of good and bad, and right and wrong, and so on. It is creative because it allows for changing those judgments when they are no longer useful. Based on this concept, there is a way to love one another that works, that is simple, and that doesn't take a lot of effort. The trouble is, it usually isn't easy.

It's easy to love people who make us feel good. It's easy to love a smiling baby, children playing happily, or helpful adults. It can be very hard to love a screaming baby, destructive children, or arrogant adults. It might be nice to be able to step instantly into unconditional love, but it is more practical to think in terms of expanding our love from where it is now, maybe even by just a little bit at a time. Like the idea that a long journey begins with the first step, the road to loving one another can start with one instance of more tolerance, or one unrewarded act of kindness.

The experience of learning how to love one another may be active or passive. Active loving is doing something for the benefit of someone else. There can be personal benefit in it, too, but for it to be called active loving the intent to benefit another must be the main reason for doing it. Many things we do out of habit or obligation could become acts of love if we would only think of whom we are benefiting by doing them. Even paying bills or paying taxes could become acts of love if, when you paid them, you thought of all the food and shelter and clothing you were providing to individuals and families dependent on your payments. Inhaling could be an act of love if you do it with the thought of giving oxygen to your cells, and exhaling could be an act of love if you do it with the thought of feeding the plants of the world.

Passive loving starts with tolerance and slowly moves its way up to appreciation. The way to increase tolerance is to start eliminating some of your rules. Almost everyone has rules about right and wrong, good and bad, possible and impossible, etcetera and etcetera. When someone breaks one of our rules we tend to get upset and either nurse our anger, criticize the rule-breaker or commit violence against them as punishment. Sometimes we do all three. The rules that have this effect most often contain the words "should" or "shouldn't." It's quite easy to get upset or angry with someone who should have done something and didn't, or who should not have done something and did. I have at various times in my life become upset with someone who was not on time for a meeting, or with someone who did not complete a task that I wanted them to do.

It's bad enough when we have too many of our own "should" and "shouldn't" rules, but we move into absurdity when we start taking on other people's rules of that kind. A few years ago I caught myself getting angry because someone was walking on a pathway on a golf course reserved for golf carts, even though there was a sign forbidding it. When I realized what I was doing I was shocked at my own behavior. In the first place, it wasn't even my golf course. In the second place, the person was neither harming nor endangering anyone else. What I discovered was that I had a very important rule that said people should not break other people's rules. Far from being useful, it was making me unnecessarily intolerant, and giving me unnecessary stress. I got rid of that rule, but I did keep the one I have about not doing things that are obviously dangerous or harmful to innocent bystanders. However, that's my rule, and it doesn't matter whether anyone else has a similar rule or not. So I am no longer a watchdog for other people's rules.

There's a very funny thing about loving one another. It gets easier to do the more you love yourself, both actively and passively. In the Bible commandment to "Love thy neighbor as thyself," there is an assumed pre-condition that most people miss. Almost everyone focuses on the "Love thy neighbor" part. I'm going to ask you to focus on the "as thyself" part for a moment. Whether you think of it as a commandment or just a good idea, "love thy neighbor as thyself" implies that you love yourself first, because that is the reference you are given for loving your neighbor (which means anyone in your vicinity, by the way). The implication is also that you think well of yourself, because if you hated yourself you would hate your neighbor. I have to admire how cleverly the author of these words incorporated the necessity for self esteem into such a short guideline for human relationships.

Having said that, in regard to one particular relationship I firmly believe that it is wise and right and good to get as close to unconditional love as we possibly can, and that relationship is with oneself. I believe this because in my experience the more you love yourself unconditionally the happier and more effective you will be in all circumstances.

Loving yourself unconditionally is more important than trying to love anyone else unconditionally. If you can't love yourself unconditionally, forget about trying to do that for someone else. You're going to fall short, and then you're going to feel bad about yourself for falling short. You are the first one to try and love unconditionally. If you start loving yourself unconditionally, then other people will begin to respond to you in that way. As a very practical aspect of this, the more you love yourself, honestly and sincerely, without needing to compare yourself to anyone else, the less you will be criticized by anyone.

There is a fact of existence that you would do well to understand. In this life of yours—speaking of parents, friends, strangers, or anyone—there will be some people who will love you depending on what you do, there will be some people who will not love you depending on what you do, there will be some people who will love you no matter what you do, and there will be some people who will not love you no matter what you do. And some of each of these people may change their minds at any time.

It makes no sense, therefore, to put your whole sense of being loved or loveable, having self esteem or self worth, and feeling accepted or connected entirely in the hands of other people. Nor does it make sense to rely on others for forgiveness of your faults and mistakes. If people do love you and like you and forgive you, that's nice. But you don't have to let your happiness depend on it.

Self love is equal to self forgiveness. And self love in the sense of simply acknowledging your own goodness, reminding yourself of it, telling it to yourself frequently, is something you can do whenever you choose. You can do it in front of a mirror if you like, but you don't have to wait until you are in front of a mirror. Do it anytime. If you get angry at yourself, just say, "Oh, that's okay, I love you anyway." If you make a mistake about something, say, "Oh, that's okay, don't worry about it, I love you anyway." If you start getting mad at someone and storm and rage and go into a funk, as soon as you can become aware say, "Oh, that doesn't matter, I love you anyway." You will be beautifully surprised at how quickly you start to come out of the negative feelings and how easily it can become a habit.

A self forgiveness exercise. This exercise is actually called *ho'oponopono iki* in Hawaiian. *Ho'oponopono* is a very ancient practice that evolved as a means of family therapy and group reconciliation, as well as a means of harmonizing any kind of relationship. I go into great detail about this technique in my book, *Instant Healing*. The more or less standard format for this technique involves a leader for the group, but the form that I am going to present now is a simple way of doing it for yourself.

1. Take a deep breath and let your body relax as best you can.

2. As you inhale, say your own name mentally.

3. As you exhale you say, "I release you," or "I forgive you." You can also be as specific as you like. If your name is Shirley, you might say something like, "Shirley… I forgive you for what you did at the party last night."

4. Do the whole process, combining breath and statements, at least three times, or until you feel better about yourself.

We create the reality of our own experience. This is not something esoteric, this is something very practical and down to earth, because one of the most important ways in which we create our experience is by our attitudes and reactions to people and things and places. Therefore, if we create our own feelings of misery and pain, we can also create our own feelings of freedom and happiness. And one of the ways to do that is by forgiving ourselves and forgiving others.

PART TWO

Your Most Intimate Relationships

CHAPTER FOUR
YOUR RELATIONSHIP WITH YOUR BODY

You might find it odd that we are talking about your body in a book on relationships, but that is your earliest, most intimate relationship, even closer than the one with your mother. As a human being, you live by means of your body, and you die by means of your body. And it is the state of your body that has the greatest influence on all the rest of your relationships, because it affects how you behave toward others, and how they behave toward you.

Since this is such an important relationship, I'm going to start by helping you to get to know your body better.

Body Awareness

Probably the most important function of your body is breathing. I say this because it's the one function you can do without the least, and the one most people know the least about.

The primary purpose of breathing seems to be simple enough: to provide your body with enough oxygen to keep your cells alive and well; and to provide a means for expelling gaseous toxins. You can read the details about that in any good book on physiology, however. I'm more interested in having you become more aware of your breathing.

Do you know how often you breathe when you are not thinking about it? Do you know how deeply you breathe when you are not putting your attention on it? Do you notice that you start to breathe more deeply and more frequently when you read or hear someone speak about breathing? Have you ever realized that your breathing becomes more shallow when you are under stress, especially when you are afraid or angry? Do you know that different parts of your body tighten up or relax, depending on how you breathe? Did you know that other people notice, consciously or subconsciously, the effects of your breathing on your body, and that they react to that by changing their behavior?

Maybe you know some of that, or none of that. It's all worth knowing. If you already knew all of that, then you are a rare individual.

The "normal" breathing rate for adults at rest is about twelve breaths per minute. Perhaps because of my training in various breathing techniques, mine are about half that. However, "normal" rates of anything are usually taken from "average" rates, and average numbers of anything are just all the numbers you have added together and divided by two. So what's really normal for one person may be quite different for someone else. More important than the rate, though, is the depth. In other words, breathing in a way that causes more oxygen to enter your system. If your breathing is very shallow, then a lot of your breathing effort is wasted, because the air never gets to the part of your body where the oxygen can be absorbed. So you can have a nice, normal breathing rate of twelve breaths per minute, and all the while your body is not getting enough oxygen and the toxins are building up. Aside from the strictly physical effects of this, regular inadequate breathing will make you more prone to anxiety and irritation, both of which will have definite effects on your other relationships.

A Conscious Breathing Exercise. There are many, many breathing techniques taught around the world for physical health, skill training, mental creativity, spiritual development, and whatever other reason human beings can think up. Well, I'm not going to give you a special breathing technique right now (maybe later). The purpose of this exercise is simply to increase your awareness of your own breathing and its effects on your mind and body.

1. Breathe any way you like, and be aware of what you are doing. You don't have to use any particular pattern or counting system. In all likelihood, though, you will probably spontaneously begin to breathe more deeply and even sigh more often. Keep this up for at least one minute.

2. In addition to the breathing itself, pay attention to anything that happens or changes in your body. Notice internal feelings and sensations, tension or relaxation, energy level, changes in your thoughts, etc. Shift your attention to different parts of your body, from head to toes, in order to increase your awareness of what is happening.

3. Practice changing your breathing pattern in any way you choose and notice how that affects your body or your feelings.

4. Practice changing your breathing pattern when you are with other people and notice whether they change their behavior in any way.

5. Generally speaking, breathing more slowly and more deeply more often will help you to feel calmer and more confident.

Movement Awareness

How you move your body also affects how you feel and how other people behave toward you. Movement includes what we usually consider as movement, of course, but in this case it also includes "static movement," or posture.

First of all, let's consider movement itself. One way to become aware of your own movement patterns is to observe how other people move. This will automatically help you to pay more attention to how you move. Watch how other people sit down and get up, how they reach for things and pick them up or handle them. Watch their hands: where do they put them when they speak or when they are quiet, what do they touch and how often and when, how do they shake hands, etc. For an interesting experience, watch someone walking in a group or a crowd and notice whether he or she is a bouncer, a glider, or a swayer. Once you look at a few people walking you'll know exactly what I mean. If you can, watch yourself in home movies so you can observe your own patterns.

Many people are not even aware of where their body is or what it is doing at any given moment. This can make them seem awkward even when they don't feel awkward, or it can actually make them awkward and more accident-prone. In the professions of acting, dancing, athletics, or martial arts this wouldn't do at all. To help increase movement awareness, some traditions and teachings have introduced various "centering" techniques. The one I'm about to introduce in the next exercise comes from my adoptive Hawaiian family. As far as I know I've only written briefly about this technique in my book, Instant Healing, and I've never written down the history of it. Since it has a strong bearing on body relationships, I'll tell the story now.

The story of *piko-piko*. A long time ago in old Hawaii, before Captain Cook, Hawaiians used to greet each other with the words, "*Pehea ko piko?*" This meant, literally, "How is your navel?" The real meaning was actually much more profound. In addition to "navel," the word, *piko*, can also refer to the crown of the head, or to the genitals. Since the crown of the head symbolized the connection to one's ancestors, the navel symbolized one's connection to one's current family, and the genitals symbolized the connection to one's descendants, the question, "*Pehea ko piko?*" really meant, "How are your relationships to these parts of your body, and to the relationships that they represent?" Unfortunately, the missionaries didn't like any questions that included the genitals or the ancestors, so today we are left with the very bland greeting, "*Pehea 'oe?*" "How are you?"

The essential meaning of *piko* is "center." Because it is associated with relationships, a technique for healing relationships called *piko-piko* grew up in my Hawaiian family and was taught to me. It's basically a technique that involves focused attention and breathing, and I will give several variations for use in healing relationships throughout the book. Meanwhile, here is a variation for relaxing the body that covers all the basics:

> 1. Inhale with your attention placed on the crown of your head.
>
> 2. Exhale with your attention on your navel.
>
> 3. Repeat as desired.

I know, I know, it seems awfully simple. But it does work. In the next exercise the variation used is even more simple.

A conscious movement exercise. The purpose of this exercise is to help you become more aware of your body while it is in motion, and to give you a way to stay centered and balanced in your body at the same time.

> 1. Do piko-piko on your navel. That is, begin by breathing with your attention on your navel as you inhale and exhale.

2. Start moving around in your present environment, slowly, and with complete conscious awareness of every movement and every part of your body that is moving.

3. Pay attention to your balance, your sensations, your feelings, and your thoughts.

4. Try putting your attention somewhere else as you move and notice any differences in how you move, how you feel, and how you think.

5. Repeat this experience on different occasions in different places. When you are with other people, move normally, but stay centered and aware. Notice any differences in other people's behavior when you are centered and aware of your body, and when you are not.

Sensory Awareness

I would venture to say that most people take it for granted that their five senses of touch, taste, smell, sound, and sight are giving them a direct experience of the world around them. It may come as somewhat of a shock to many people, therefore, that such an assumption is no more than a childlike fantasy.

Our organs of sensing receive information, that's true, but then they convert it into an electrical signal that travels along the pathways of our nervous system by means of neurons, or nerve cells. The information, whatever it is, is passed along from one nerve cell to another, but not directly. Between each nerve cell is a small gap where the information is converted into a different form and handed over to tiny molecules called neurotransmitters that carry it across the gap, convert it again, and pass it on to the next nerve cell. Eventually the information reaches its destination where, if the information is important enough, it is mysteriously converted from whatever it has become into what we call "awareness."

That's probably more than you wanted to know, but the point is that a whole lot of little bits of your body are involved in any information that you get from your skin, your tongue, your nose, your ears, and your eyes. In addition, distortion of the information can happen at any point along the way, due to tension states, toxins in the body, memory associations, and other things. That's one reason why different people can process the same information and come to very different conclusions about what they are sensing, and what it means. It's like being the president of a country who is trying to find out what's going on in the world when the information given to him has been filtered through a billion or more committees. It really is a miracle that we can function at all on this planet, or that we can communicate as well as we do with other people.

Nevertheless, as long as we are getting the information the way we are, we may as well learn how to increase the amount of information we get in order to become more effective at relating to other people who have to do it in the same way.

Your Sense Of Touch

Your sense of touch operates through your skin, and your skin is your largest sensory organ. It's actually your largest organ of any kind, taking up about 16% or your whole body mass. I'm not going to go into a lot of detail about how it functions, but three things about it are important in terms of relationships:

1. It is your most immediate and direct means of contact with other people and with the rest of the world.

2. It is packed with nerve cells that send messages directly (more or less) to your brain.

3. Around the nerves and around the hairs on your skin is a lot of muscle tissue that tightens up under physical, emotional, and mental stress, and one of the important results of that is a diminishing of your sensitivity to and awareness of any information related to your sense of touch.

The phenomenon of being "out of touch" with people is a based on the actual effect of skin tension being high enough to block awareness of sensory input. I have worked with people who had suffered from sexual, physical, emotional, or mental abuse. In a good number of cases these people not only had diminished awareness of touch, their skin had a drum-like tightness that made any skin-related sensory input painful. For some of them, even putting conscious attention on their own skin was too much to bear. As various means were used to relieve their skin tension, means that mainly had to do with changing their thinking patterns about other people, their tolerance for touch increased and their relationships with people improved.

Your sense of touch is not limited to physical contact with someone or something, although tense skin will also limit the amount of information you can get from that source. Your skin is sensitive as well to air pressure, temperature, electromagnetic fields, light, and what some people call "subtle energy," which can come from electromagnetic or bioenergetic fields. The most sensitive areas of your body are your tongue, lips, face, neck, hands, fingertips, and feet. The part of your body that is least sensitive to touch is the middle of your back.

Normally, touching the skin has a great many more benefits than mere sensation. Research shows that children who are touched a lot develop stronger immune systems, grow more quickly, are more emotionally stable, are more alert and active, sleep more soundly, develop movement earlier, and have larger brains than those who receive little or no touch.

70

Studies with adults demonstrate that massage releases endorphins, natural chemicals in the body that ease pain and produce a feeling of wellbeing. Other studies suggest that people can even learn to distinguish colors through their skin, and project a healing influence to others.

Tense skin, however, can inhibit all of these benefits. While the services of a professional masseur or masseuse would be very helpful, and the hug or caress of a friend or lover might be even better, you don't have to wait for the right occasion because you can go ahead and touch yourself and still get most of the benefits.

A simple self-touch exercise. This exercise is probably best done on bare skin, but your skin will still feel touched even if you do it over clothing.

>   1. Be as daring or as modest as you choose, and give your skin a light brushing with your hands. At the very least, include your entire head, your neck and shoulders, stomach and whatever part of your back you can reach, hips, and legs, and feet.
>   2. Give an individual squeeze to each and every finger and toe.
>   3. Using two or three fingers of either hand, touch and vibrate the skin over the center of your chest, the area on your hands where your thumb and forefinger meet, and on the little bone that sticks out at the top of your spine.

You can do this as frequently as you like, even partially, to help yourself relax, calm down, and get ready to better enjoy the company of others.

The Sense Of Taste

Although wonderful in and of itself, this sense has little to do with relationships, except in certain intimate situations or when you don't like the taste of what a host has served you. Also, about eighty percent of what we taste is due to our perception of how it smells. Therefore, I'm going to pass on any more discussion of it.

The Sense Of Smell

Your sense of smell plays an extremely important role in your relationships, because when you smell someone's odor you are actually taking a piece of that person's body into your own body and analyzing the smell itself as well as how it makes you feel.

That's right. As disgusting as that might sound, we detect odors by inhaling airborne bits of things all the way to the back of our noses, where the molecules involved settle into special nerve cells. At that point, as with all our senses, the information about the molecule gets transformed into an electrical signal and starts the familiar neuron-synapse-neuron process toward the brain, but what happens there is anyone's guess. Relatively little research has been done on the physiology of smell since sight and sound took over as the most important senses of "civilized" people in the nineteenth century. For instance, science writers will often say that humans are capable of detecting 10,000 different odors, but that figure is a wild guess (technically called an "assumption") made by some scientists without any research to back it up. What is known is that professional "noses" (people who smell perfumes and wines for a living) are supposed to be able to distinguish 3000 different odors before graduating from special schools.

More is known about the sense of smell and human behavior, and we'll concentrate on the relationship aspect of that in this section.

First of all, a few words about how important the sense of smell is in some cultures around the world.

The Serer tribe in Senegal associate personal identity

with odor, believing in two forces defined by scent: a physical one related to the body and the odor of breath; and a spiritual odor that reincarnates in a descendant. Indeed, they claim to be able to recognize a reincarnated ancestor by the smell of a child.

Among the Desana of the Amazon, it is believed that all members of a tribe have a similar odor, and marriages are only allowed between people who smell different.

Instead of anything that we would call perfume, the Dassanetch of Ethiopia think that nothing smells better than cows, so as a sign of social status and to attract members of the opposite sex, the men smear themselves with manure and the women cover their upper bodies with butter.

For Ongee people of the Andaman Islands in the Bay of Bengal off the coast of India, everything in the universe is defined by smell, including personal identity. An Ongee refers to himself by touching the tip of his nose to indicate both "me" and "my odor." Instead of saying, "How are you?" he would say, "How is your nose?"

In the Hawaiian language there are sixty-four words related to smell in the current dictionary, and there may have been more in the distant past. A traditional greeting that can still be seen or experienced today is the *honi*, usually described as "to touch noses on the side as a greeting." However, the word, *honi*, also means "to smell, to sniff," and every traditional Hawaiian that I have exchanged this greeting with makes sure that sniffing is part of the process. At some point there were undoubtedly criteria for determining the character or origin of whomever you were sniffing. What is also known is that the ancient Hawaiians went out of their way to scent their clothing and bedding with pleasant, natural perfumes, and even considered some fragrances as food for the gods.

Modern Western society and smell. Let's start with

dispelling some myths. Men, take note: studies show that most women definitely do not like the smell of male sweat, especially if it's been hanging on his body for more than a few minutes. Women, take note: studies also show that most men couldn't care less about what perfume you are wearing, no matter how expensive it is, unless it is too strong or just smells bad to them. Individual men will have their preferences, of course, and men who specialize in seduction will go out of their way to learn how to identify all the most popular scents by name and manufacturer.

Oh, yes, one of the biggest myths is that if you just dab on a perfume with the right kind of pheromone in it you can make the opposite sex go crazy over you. Pheromones are chemicals emitted by some animals, including insects, specifically for the purpose of sexual attraction. In mammals, these un-scented chemicals are perceived by special glands in the nose that are unrelated to smell receptors. In spite of marketing claims, the current state of research on pheromones and humans is such that scientists are not even sure these glands are functional in human beings, and do not know how they would function if they were active.

Even though the sense of smell is underrated and underutilized in modern society (not counting the cosmetics industry), the ability to distinguish odors in modern people has not atrophied. Experiments have shown that both men and women are able to recognize their own spouses and children by scent, even by the scent of their clothes.

Some simple practices with smell. Here are a few things that will help you smell better.

1. It is well know by "noses" and trackers, among others, that the more attention you pay to odors, the greater the number of different odors you are able to identify. If you want to increase this ability in order to enhance your relationships, practice smelling your own body and your own clothes, then

extend your practice to other people. Sniffing other people is rather impolite in modern society, so just inhale gently when you are near them.

2. Other experiments have shown that men who wear colognes that they like and women who wear perfumes that they like experience mood-improvements in ways that have a positive effect on their relationships. This strongly suggests that wearing a scent that you like may be much better for your relationships than wearing what you think someone else might like.

3. Don't forget the basics. Clean bodies are generally nicer to associate with, scented or un-scented.

The Sense Of Hearing

There is so much about the human body that is miraculous, and right near the top of the list has to be our sense of hearing. With a sense organ about the size of a pea we are able to locate, distinguish, and process sounds that come from different sources and that vibrate at different frequencies. Not only that, but this organ is able to take responsibility for our sense of balance at the same time.

The way it works is almost unbelievable. Sound waves come through the air and hit your outer ear (the part that some of you would like to be smaller, and some of you wish were closer to your head). The outer ear channels the sound waves into the inner ear where they cause your eardrum to vibrate. This causes a hammer bone to hit an anvil bone that hits a stirrup bone that hits another type of drum that causes waves in a liquid to move little hairs that change the vibrational information to electrical signals that hop and skip their way to the brain. And without even thinking you are able to instantly tell the difference between a whisper and thunder.

Those sound waves are not a direct experience of the source of sound, however. When you speak to another person you are vibrating your larynx and manipulating your mouth, tongue, and lips in such a way as to send modulated waves through the air between you, hoping that the other person's sound receiver system can interpret the information carried by those waves in the way you want them to.

More than any of the other senses, your sense of hearing is very dependent on your mental concentration. If you stop concentrating on a particular sound it can disappear completely from your conscious awareness, even if it is quite loud.

Sometimes this is a good thing. When my wife and I lived in Senegal we had a villa on a peninsula called "La Corniche." We were happy with that until we discovered that our home was directly in line with the last landing phase of the passenger jets coming into the Dakar Airport. At times it sounded, and felt, as if the wheels of the planes were rolling on our roof. I don't recall how long it took for us to get used to it, but I do remember having guests over one night and being surprised during a conversation at the sudden, startled look on their faces as they stared upward. It took a conscious effort to bring the jet noise back into my awareness so I could sympathize with them.

Sometimes it is not such a good thing, such as when you are talking to an important, but boring, person and your attention drifts away while they are saying something that they believe is significant.

Being able to hear what a person is actually saying, rather than what you think they might be saying can make or break a relationship. Because we have this ability to tune out as well as to tune in sounds, it frequently happens that two people speaking to each other are each having a one-way conversation. If you would like to improve your ability to tune in at will, here are two practice exercises.

Concentrated Hearing - Exercise One: The purpose of

this exercise is to help you experience the effect of shifting your attention while listening to one source of sound.

1. Pick out some music that you like and play it. Just listen to it like you normally would.

2. While the song is still playing, put your attention in the center of your head as you maintain your awareness of the song. Do this for about 30 seconds and feel how that feels.

3. In the same way, shift your attention for 30 seconds at a time to the center of your chest, your stomach, your hands, and your ears.

4. The next time you have an extended conversation with someone, try this and experience the effect.

Concentrated Hearing – Exercise Two: The purpose of this one is to help you expand your awareness of more than one sound at a time. For instance, as I'm writing this I am aware of the sound of my computer keys, the sound of my noisy computer itself, the sound of a neighbor mowing his lawn, and the sound of my tendons rubbing over my bones as I turn my head.

1. In whatever environment you are in, focus your attention on hearing itself, and how many different sounds you can hear around you and inside you.

2. Practice with a particular type of sound, like wind, or water, or traffic, and count how many different sounds you can hear within the main source. You might be surprised.

The Sense of Sight

Did you know that you are not really looking at anything you are seeing? That's a fact of life, and there isn't anything you can do about it, because your sense of sight comes from the ability of your eyes to perceive reflected light. In practical terms, if you are looking at a friend or a lover, what you are seeing is only whatever frequency ranges of light energy are not being absorbed by that person's body or clothing. If people didn't reflect any light, they would either appear pitch black (if they absorbed all the light energy) or invisible (if they let it all pass through them). Reflected light is a pretty indirect way of seeing anyone or anything, but it's all we have and most of us have to make do with it.

Of course, it's not that simple. Light rays don't just go right through your eyes to your brain. There's a whole lot of room for distortion before you become aware of what or whom you see.

The process of seeing begins with light entering the cornea of your eye, a rather thick, protective, and transparent layer of cells that covers your whole eye. Then light passes through your pupil, the dark spot in the center that is really just a hole to let light through, adjusted in size by the colored muscle around it called the iris. Next, the light moves on through a lens, passes through a substance like jelly, and finally reaches that back of the eye to land on a surface called the retina. Science writers love to tell you that the image you are receiving is projected onto the retina upside down, like on a movie screen, but this is totally misleading. The retina is made up of a whole lot of cells sensitive to light divided into two types called rods and cones. The rods help you to recognize shapes, and they work best in dim lighting. The cones help you to recognize colors, and they work best in bright light. Both of these cells combine their information, convert it into electrical signals, and send it through the optic nerve system to the brain, which does its mysterious thing so you can see. Even more mysterious is the fact that, according to very recent research, there are enormous variations between people in the distribution of the color sensitive cone cells of their eyes, yet remarkably similar experiences of color. And that's the simple explanation.

Distortion of the information you are getting from the light source can happen in many different ways. There are a lot of muscles in and around the eye, and the more tension the muscles have, the more it becomes harder to see clearly. This can make a big difference in how well a relationship functions, especially if you can't tell whether a person is happy or sad, along with all the other, more subtle, visual signs of emotional states that people convey, consciously and subconsciously. For instance, my wife tells me that I give a very slight twitch to one side of my nose when I don't want to do something, and on her face I notice a "look," a particular, indefinable expression that tells me when she doesn't want to do something. If our vision isn't clear enough we miss out on all those little signs.

A simple exercise to ease eye tension. This exercise can provide temporary or permanent eye tension relief, depending on how much and how often you do it. My father-in-law did it extensively for three months and threw away his glasses at age fifty and never wore nor needed glasses again until his death at ninety-one. I use it occasionally when I need to read the fine print on a vitamin bottle. If there are emotional reasons why your eyes are tense, this will provide temporary relief only.

1. Squeeze your eyes shut five times in a row.
2. Look at something and try to feel or imagine that your pupil is expanding.
3. Repeat as desired.

A very different kind of visual distortion can occur because of your brain's ability to make up things. I'm not talking about mental fantasies; I'm talking about hallucination, the apparent experience of sensory input that isn't really "out there."

Your brain has this ability because it does it all the time, due to an oddity in the way mammalian eyes are constructed.

79

Remember the optic nerve mentioned above? Well, instead of being nicely positioned off to the side as in octopus eyes, in mammals it is attached directly to the retina, displacing a certain number of rods and cones without caring about the consequences. As a result, everyone—and that means everyone—has a literal blind spot in each eye, a place where light isn't registered at all. Unless something could compensate for this, we would all "see" a black hole from each eye as we look around, which would be very inconvenient. So the brain compensates by creating the illusion that we can see something when we really can't.

How to find your blind spot. There are a number of different ways to demonstrate this, but I've chosen one that is the most portable.

> 1. Stand or sit and find an object straight ahead of you at eye level to look at that is farther away than the length of your arm.
> 2. Look at this object, extend your left arm out and raise your thumb in front of the object at about the level of your nose, and close your right eye.
> 3. Keeping your left eye on the object, slowly move your thumb horizontally to the left until the top of your thumb disappears. This is your physical blind spot. You can do the same thing with your left eye and your right thumb. The exact location of this spot will vary with individuals.

However, if this sounds too complicated, use the image below to experience the same effect:

Hold the image about 20 inches or 50 centimeters away from you and close your right eye. Look at the + with your left eye and slowly bring the image closer. When it reaches a certain distance, the dot will disappear because it has reached the blind spot on your retina. Try it the other way by closing your left eye, looking at the dot with your right eye, and bringing the image closer until the + disappears.

You do not see this blind spot when you look around because your brain fills in the area with information from the other data that you are looking at, thus making it seem as if your eyes are seeing everything.

Your brain uses this ability for other situations as well. In English we say that someone has a "blind spot" in relation to some experience of life when that person does not see it as everyone else does, but only as they think it ought to be. Various psycho-physiological experiments have demonstrated this ability of the brain to change data to fit expectations. In one such experiment subjects saw and recorded black aces of spades and red eights of hearts projected on a movie screen, when the actual projection was of red aces of spades and black eights of hearts. In another experiment a man was fitted with special glasses that turned the world upside down to his sight. He wore them night and day, and on the third day, in spite of the glasses, his brain turned the world right side up again.

In dealing with other people we sometimes project our expectations onto them without really seeing who they are. Parents may see their adult progeny as the little children they once were, instead of who they have become. Women who have been hurt by men and men who have been hurt by women may see all members of the opposite sex as replicas of the one who hurt them. Judges may see criminals as potential good citizens, no matter how terrible their crimes. And people may see stereotypes of race or religion, instead of individual human beings. I remember talking about this with a fellow sergeant in the United States Marine Corps. The man was very upset and confused because his personal experience of "blacks" (the appropriate term current at the time for people of African descent) in our unit was good, but his learned experience handed down through his family was that they were bad. It is the brain that creates these experiences, fed by fear, desire, and, naturally, sensory information.

A technique for clearing unwanted hallucinations. This technique will only work if you really want to see through the fog of expectation, if you have any. It will not get rid of expectations, it will simply give you another perception for you to choose from.

1. Start with a decision to act as if, for any period of time you decide on, that this is your very first day on Earth. The only knowledge you have is how to speak the languages you've learned. Most especially, pretend you have no memories associated with any other human being except, perhaps, their relationship to you. That relationship, however, is what it is in the present moment and has no history.

2. Encounter or think about a person currently in your life. If the person is present, speak to him or her and observe behavior, but do not refer to anything in the past or in the future, because, for now, that information is not available. Also, for the same reason, do not compare that person to anyone else, not even to a vision of what he or she could be, and especially not to what he or she might have done in the past, because that does not exist while this technique is being used. If the person is not present, just remember the person's behavior without trying to interpret it, like an anthropologist doing raw research.

3. Pay attention to your feelings while doing this, and to how easy or difficult it seems. Most of all, see if you can learn anything you did not know before.

What's Next?

Next, we'll explore the role of your mind in your relationships.

CHAPTER FIVE
YOUR RELATIONSHIP WITH YOUR MIND

How can you have a relationship with something as insubstantial as the mind? Most people in the scientific community do not even like to admit that there is such a thing as the mind. Their idea of the "mind/body" connection is that the mind is an effect of the body, the brain in particular. In spite of that, they have no idea how a physical experience, like sensation, can become a mental experience, or how a thought can transform itself into a physical effect.

Most normal people know that even though the state of the body can affect the state of the mind, and that the state of the mind can affect the state of the body, there are still large and important areas of our experience that are not physical at all. Imagination and fantasy, recall and expectations, speculation and reasoning, the list can go on and on. Nevertheless, the mind remains difficult to define. One fairly decent definition from Webster's Encyclopedic Unabridged Dictionary of the English Language says that, "Mind is that part of a man which thinks, feels, and wills." Not bad, but the word "think" is still pretty vague, even in this dictionary, because it's used to cover so many different things. And then there's the problem with the act of thinking itself. We think thoughts. We think about thoughts. We think thoughts about things and we think about the thoughts that we have about things. And we also think about thinking. That approach isn't going to lead us to anything useful.

I'm going to cut through all the problems with a radically different definition of the mind, and the phenomenon of thinking. First, though, I'm going to define the body as that part of human beings which senses, remembers, and moves. That brings us to my definition of the mind: that part of human beings which perceives, recalls, and imagines. The act of thinking, by this definition, is simply the act of perceiving, recalling, and imagining.

Even as I write this I can mentally hear all the objections. Or am I just imagining that? Anyway, let me explain why I chose this definition, and then how it will help you to establish a better relationship with your own mind, which will then help you with your other relationships, too.

The Perceiving Mind

The body senses and the mind perceives. What's the difference? In the current context, sensing is the purely physical operation of receiving information through the sensory organs, converting that information into electrical signals, passing the converted information on to the brain and/or other parts of the body, and storing the information in some manner (we are not going to discuss the storage system in this book).

In contrast, perceiving is the purely mental operation of becoming aware of information, whether it comes from your sensory organs or any other source. This perception might take the form of visual, auditory, kinesthetic, or other kinds of awareness.

An exercise in perception. This exercise is designed to help you perceive things in a slightly different way, with the idea that, eventually, it will help you to perceive people in a slightly different way.

> 1. Touch as many things as you can that are within your reach. Be aware of differences in texture and temperature.
>
> 2. Listen to all the sounds around you. Be aware of differences in pitch (highness or lowness), loudness, and quality (a computer sounds different than a fan, which sounds different than a bird).
>
> 3. Look at the different shapes of things, at the spaces between objects, and their colors. Try to find all the colors of the rainbow, plus white and black.

Perceptual Frameworks. As I said above, perceiving is not the same as sensing, because perception involves interpretation of what we are sensing. Interpretation is always based on rules, which will be discussed later, and most often on "rule sets" or frameworks that we are seldom consciously aware of.

For instance, you may perceive some people from within the framework of being a customer or a client, an employee or an employer, a student or a teacher, and your relationships with them will be modified by your perception. Furthermore, your perceptual framework will also affect how much of your sensory environment you perceive. If you are not sure about that last part, try this experiment:

> 1. Wherever you are, look around at your environment as if you were a photographer. Be aware of what you see and how you see it.
>
> 2. In the same way, look at your environment as if you were a landscape artist (outside) or an interior designer (inside).

3. In the same way again, look around as if you were a farmer (outside) or a carpenter (inside).

If you pay close attention you will notice that each change in your perceptual framework makes certain things important and other things unimportant. As you change frameworks, some things draw your attention and other things fade into the background or out of your perception entirely. The same thing happens when we perceive people from different frameworks. The more narrow the framework, such as that of a stereotype, the less we perceive of what is actually there.

There is another kind of perception that receives information from sources other than the ordinary senses as we usually think of them.

Extended Perception. You may prefer to call it "intuition" or "hunches," but the fact remains that we often perceive information about other people that cannot be explained by conventional ideas about physiology and consciousness. Without going into where such information might originate in this book, it nevertheless plays a very important role in all relationships. Sometimes this kind of perception takes the form of mental imagery, sometimes what can be called mental sound, sometimes a peculiar sense of "knowing," and often an unexplainable "feeling" that may be pleasant or unpleasant, attractive or repelling. Any of these perceptions may influence either our reactions or our actions in regard to other people, and so they ought to be taken into account.

The Recalling Mind

A lot of our thinking time is taken up with recalling events and experiences. Please note that I am making an important distinction here between remembering and recalling. By my definition, it is the body that remembers, literally. As needed, or stimulated, it puts together scattered records of sensory experience and re-enacts them in the present moment. Sometimes this involves the mind and sometimes it doesn't.

There are a lot of physical and emotional actions, reactions, and habits that people engage in without thinking about it. You may smile automatically when you see someone you like, or frown without even realizing it when you hear the voice of someone you don't like. You body may drive your car for you while you converse with a friend, and under certain circumstances you may laugh or cry without intending to, because your body reacts to something it has smelled or heard or seen that is below the level of your conscious perception.

At the same time, you may purposely recall a list of tasks that you are supposed to do, bring experiences back into your awareness when you look at a photograph or watch a home movie, call up the words and music of a song you want to sing to someone, or spontaneously think of a long past event when you smell a particular odor.

Your recall ability is most evident when you recognize things, like people's faces and voices. It is also very evident when you speak to someone, because in the act of speaking you are recalling not only how to speak, but also the grammar and vocabulary you need to express what you want to say.

Typically, when you recall an event, like a party, you first recall the specific happening that made the most impression on you, emotionally or physically. Maybe you first recall the eyes of a nice person you met, or the drink someone spilled on you, or a particular piece of music. The longer you keep your attention on the party, the more specific happenings you recall, until, in assorted order, you recall pretty much the whole party. On the other hand, your mind also has the ability to impose a chronological order on the recall, but that takes more concentration. Like any talent, the more you practice detailed recall, the better you get at it, and the more able you are to recall other talents and skills, as well as information.

An exercise in recall. This is the type of exercise you can do to gain the benefits mentioned above. Use the suggestions given here, or do it your way. The more time you give each recall, the more details will come forth.

> 1. Recall the first pretty girl or handsome boy you ever saw, or the earliest one you can. What did he or she really look like? Hair color? Eye color? Clothing? Movement? Voice? Location?
>
> 2. Recall your first kiss. Who was it with? How did it feel? Were the other person's lips warm or cool? Was it just a kiss, or was there touching, too? Was it daytime or nighttime? Did you like or not?
>
> 3. Recall the best dinner out you ever had with someone. Where was it? What did you eat and drink? How did it taste? What was the waiter or waitress like? Was there any music? Who paid the bill?

I briefly mentioned the recognition of faces above. Let's look at that in more detail.

Pattern Recognition. If you recall, I wrote at some length about the hole in your vision and how your brain fills it in. This has very far-reaching consequences for many things in your life, including your relationships. Recognizing someone's face comes from the stimulation of a remembered pattern of shape and color and, sometimes, movement. Recognizing someone from behind at a distance requires only the stimulation of part of a remembered pattern. Your brain fills in the rest, and because of that the recognition may not be correct. In the same way, the sight or sound or smell or touch of a person may stimulate your recall of only part of a remembered behavior pattern associated with that person. If your brain fills in the rest of the pattern for your recall, you may or may not find that useful. It's like some of the new word-processing programs that fill in a word for you when you type in the first one or two letters. Sometimes that saves you time, and sometimes it wastes your time, because it isn't what you want and you have to stop and correct the mistake.

I recall as a young man going to restaurants where the waitresses prided themselves on recalling what kind of drink and meal the customer wanted. It was upsetting for them to serve me, because I always wanted something different every time I came. Even more problems occur when your expectations of a person's behavior, based on filled-in pattern recall, no longer match who that person has become. We'll cover that in another chapter, however. For now, I would like to give you an experience that demonstrates how your brain fills in patterns for you to fit remembered patterns. Although the drawing only contains broken lines, your brain gives you circles where there aren't any. The same process occurs when you see faces in clouds, or rocks, or carpets. Actually, the same process also occurs when you watch cartoons or look at impressionist paintings. It happens again when you look at images of people formed out of lots of really tiny photographs, or see images in the computer-generated dots of stereograms. And it happens in some way or another with all of the people that you know and meet.

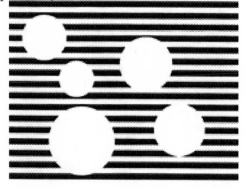

The Imagining Mind

This part of my definition may evoke the most controversy, since I have a very different view of what constitutes imagination. This is also the part of the mind's operation that has the greatest influence on relationships. In the following paragraphs I will discuss various mental activities that I consider to fall within the province of imagination.

Reasoning. The ability to reason is often thought of as the grandest of human attributes, something that sets us apart from the other animals, including our disturbingly close relatives, the chimpanzees. Cicero put it this way:

> Wise men are instructed by reason; men of less understanding, by experience; the most ignorant, by necessity; and beasts by nature.

That sounds very noble, but what does it really mean? Reasoning is usually defined as the ability to draw logical conclusions from a truth, and therein lies its weakness. The validity of the logic is entirely dependent on what is defined as truth. If a given group of people were to hold it as true that men were superior to women by their very nature, then reason would dictate that men should receive more benefits and privileges than women, no matter how competent the women in that group may be. If another group believes without a doubt that what it believes is the only possible truth, then reason would dictate that all other beliefs are false and should be ignored or suppressed.

The question before us is, where does truth come from? The answer is, from people. Individual people like you and me. Truths don't fall out of the sky. Someone has to make them up.

That's right. Someone makes them up. Do you recall what I said about rules in the first chapter? Here is how a truth is created:

1. You have an experience.

2. You make up a rule about what the experience means, usually based on recall of similar experiences or recall of what someone else has told you.

3. At this point, if you are unsure about the meaning, you call it an opinion. If you don't doubt it, you call it a truth.

4. The rule you made up about the meaning of the experience is remembered by your body and available for recall.

5. Frequently recalled opinion rules often become rules of truth.

Just to make it very clear, I'm saying that the whole process of reasoning begins with rules (some people call them assumptions) that you or someone else made up about an experience of some kind. The ability to reason is based on imagination.

Why is this so important to know? Because everything you believe about anything is based on made-up rules. All your beliefs about yourself, about relationships, about men, women, children, about all the individuals you know, are really rules. Even more importantly, the rules you have about these things affect your experience with them. If your rules are working for you, i.e., if they are affecting your relationships in a good way, then that's great. If not, then there's good news and there's bad news. The good news is, rules can be changed. The bad news is, they're a lot easier to change if you know what they are.

Actually, that's not really bad news, because I'm going to help you discover what your rules are. First I'm going to ask you to make a short list—not more than four items to begin with—of beliefs that you think you have about yourself in relation to other people, or that you would like to have. The technique I'm about to give you will help you to discover if what you think you believe is what you really believe. You'll know the difference by your reactions to the technique. It can also help you to reinforce beliefs you already have, or replace old beliefs with new ones. You can choose any belief you want to work with, but here's a sample list to get you started:

- I love myself
- People like me
- I like people
- I am attractive

Now, here's the technique:

1. Set two small bowls in front of you, side by side.

2. In one of the bowls, place 25-50 small objects, like beads, coins, or marbles.

3. One at a time, move an object from one bowl to the other bowl.

4. Each time you move an object, state a belief or a rule of your choice. Use the same statement throughout the session.

5. Repeat the process, making a statement and moving the objects back and forth between the bowls for as long as you like.

There is no way to predict what the effect of doing this will be for a particular person. If what you are saying corresponds closely with what your body remembers and feels, you may not experience much of anything. If your statement represents an idea that you like, and if it's not opposed by any strong memories, then you may feel a rising sense of excitement. If the statement is in sharp opposition to rules or beliefs that you already have, then your experience may not be fun at all, because there could be unpleasant physical, emotional, or even mental reactions. With statements like these, it is not uncommon for a feeling of tension or anxiety to occur in the chest area, but there could be other reactions, too. This is only a sign that opposing ideas exist. You can either choose not to go on and put the bowls and objects away, or you can choose to keep strengthening the idea by using the technique frequently until the new rule has become a truth for you.

Decision-making. What do decisions have to do with imagination? Everything.

Making decisions is usually considered to be a purely intellectual activity, sometimes influenced by emotions, and sometimes guided by cold logic. I hate to burst anyone's bubble, but emotions are clearly based on imagination (see the next chapter) and "cold logic," as we have seen above, begins with imagination.

Furthermore, decisions are made in the first place because you imagine that something is going to happen, and then you imagine the best way to deal with that. If you decide to write a book, for instance, it's only because there is something you imagine doing, or saying, or receiving that feels good to you. Then you imagine writing the book, and then you do it.

Many people try to separate thinking about something, deciding to do something, and doing something, but in my view they are all part of the same process. Thinking about something, which is the same thing as imagining doing it, may stir up feelings, but unless it switches on a habit or leads to the next step, there won't be any action taken. Deciding to do it, which is the same as imagining the act of doing in a concentrated way, will automatically lead to the doing if nothing else is done to inhibit it. And the only thing that could inhibit it is a decision not to do it, or a body state that does not allow the doing.

Your body always responds to your mind. Think a thought and your body immediately begins to act it out in whatever way it can. If you have established a habit (a remembered rule or set of rules) that tells your body not to fully act out what you are thinking, then your body will act it out in a partial way. You may have a mean boss and think about kicking him or her, but you may also have remembered rules that say, "No, no, no! That is bad or dangerous! Do not do that!" In this case, your body will immediately start to act out the thought of kicking your boss, getting all the muscles ready to do the job, and just as immediately stop the action by increasing tension in those muscles so that the act cannot be carried out. The more strongly you feel about the act, the more tension the body needs to generate in order to stop it. Mentally, what has happened is that you imagined doing something, and then quickly imagined not doing it.

Most people I have met or taught think of imagination as some long and drawn-out process, and sometimes it is. Sometimes, though, it happens so quickly that you don't consciously notice it. The next exercise will help you notice it more often.

An exercise in decision-making. Every physical action you perform, and every emotional reaction you feel, is preceded by a decision. And every decision is an act of imagination that stimulates your body into physical action or emotional reaction. If you think this has nothing to do with relationships, you aren't thinking.

> 1. Decide to pick up something, and pick it up. Pay very close attention to what you are thinking as you make the decision. Decide to pick up, and then pick up, several things until you can really be aware of what your mind is doing when you make the decision.
>
> 2. Decide to pick up something, and then do not pick it up. Pay very close attention to what you are thinking as you make both decision. Repeat this with several objects until you can really be aware of what your mind is doing when you make the decisions.

Concentration. Also called focus, concentration is the ability to center your attention on something. Imagination is the source of this ability, because first you imagine putting your attention on something, and then you perceive the information your senses are giving you in the area of attention. Imagination used this way generally happens so quickly you might not notice it, but if you pay attention to the process for a while it will become evident. In the absence of a physical defect or disease, the ability to narrow concentration or to broaden it comes from a combination of imagination (to move the attention), recall (about remembered rules concerning what's important and what isn't), and perception (awareness that is restricted or broad, depending on the rules).

An exercise in concentration. This will help you to become more aware of the process of changing your focus.

> 1. Look at an object that is at least ten feet or three meters away from you.
>
> 2. Become aware of some detail of that object
>
> 3. Notice how much of what is around it tends to fade out of your perception.
>
> 4. Keep your attention centered on the object, but expand your awareness of your peripheral vision.
>
> 5. Notice how many other things now come into your perception.

I can concentrate on something, like a good book or a computer game, to the exclusion of practically everything else outside the area of my restricted perception. Unfortunately, this means that sometimes I don't hear my wife calling me for dinner. On the other hand, I do a lot of teaching around the world, and I have found that it is extremely useful to maintain peripheral awareness while I teach, so that I can be aware of temperature, lighting, potential disturbances, and audience reactions. Imagination is what guides our concentration, and helps us to change our focus from narrow to broad as needed or desired.

Another exercise in concentration. This is a famous image often used to demonstrate optical illusions. I think it demonstrates the effects of shifting focus even better. Using your imagination, make the decision to go back and forth between concentrating on the black part of the image and the white part, and notice how your perception changes as a result. This type of picture was introduced in 1915 by psychologist Edgar Rubin.

Is it a vase on a black background, or two people on a white background about to kiss? It isn't either one, actually, but as you change your focus from the white part to the black part, your wonderful brain will give an image based on a remembered pattern.

Some people take advantage of this propensity on the part of your brain by using disguises that alter expectations by promoting pattern fill-in. Some things like this are clothing identified with a particular culture or sub-culture, eyeglasses or hair color identified with a particular personality type, speech patterns identified with a particular ethnic group or area, and so on. The experts in such disguises know how to make small changes that your brain interprets to your mind as big changes. Cosmetics are used in a similar way. It is astounding how different a celebrity can look with and without make-up.

Analysis. Technically, analysis is the process of studying the nature of something by separating its parts and determining their relationships in order to predict behavior in relation to something else. A man named Eric Berne developed a method of applying this to people called "Transactional Analysis." He defined a transaction as an exchange of communication between people. These exchanges were separated into positive exchanges, called "strokes," and negative exchanges, called "games," and these exchanges were analyzed in great detail. The method is still in use and has proven beneficial to many people. As is typical of analytical systems, it can get very complicated, because you never run out of things to analyze, and ways to analyze.

Much earlier, Sigmund Freud developed the system of Psychoanalysis, based on a process of analyzing three factors supposedly common to all people: the Id, the Ego, and the Super-ego. And a lot of people have benefited from that system, too. In the system of Huna psychology that I teach, we analyze the relationships between the Ku (body mind), the Lono (conscious mind), and Kane (higher self), and, needless to say, many people benefit.

However, these systems of personality or relationship analysis, and every other one there is, are all based on the imagined existence of imagined parts that can be analyzed. Different people at different times have observed human behavior and have used their imagination to arbitrarily divide that behavior into segments that can be studied. In reality, there is no Ego, no Ku, and no Transaction, unless you decide to look at human behavior that way. Likewise, there is no month of June unless you decide to divide the year up into twelve months and call one of them June. Human imagination divides up the year, not Nature. And different human beings divide things up differently. That's why the Gregorian calendar, the Jewish calendar, the Mayan calendar, and the

Hawaiian calendar are not the same.

Here's just one more example. Today we use a "scientific classification" system for use in analyzing plants and animals, including humans. Bottle-nosed dolphins are classified as being of the Class of Mammals, the Order of Cetacea (whales), the Sub-Order of Odontoceti (toothed whales), the Family of Delphinidae (all dolphins and close relatives), the Genus and Species of Tursiops truncatus (specifically, the bottle-nosed dolphin). All of this starts with their classification as mammals, which means that they share three characteristics with all other mammals: three ear bones, hair (dolphins have it, but not much), and mammary glands. So of course it's easy to tell the difference between a dolphin and a shark, right? Sharks don't have any of those three things, and in addition they breathe with gills, their tails are vertical instead of horizontal, they don't have a backbone, etc. Nevertheless, at some point someone decided—that means someone imagined—that certain characteristics about dolphins were more important than other characteristics. And from that initial assumption an extremely logical system for analyzing the place of dolphins in zoology came about. In different times, under different circumstances, the ancient Hawaiians saw dolphins differently. Their system was far less complicated, but based on what they imagined was important they classified dolphins with sharks. After all, both of them have vertical dorsal fins, both of them have teeth, both of them give birth to live young, both of them gather in groups, both of them surf, etc. Our modern classification system is the most popular one, but that doesn't mean that it's the only possible one that there is.

My main point in all of this is that even an intellectual process like analysis is based on imagination. First you imagine that certain characteristics about something are important. Then you invent a classification system based on those characteristics. Then you observe members of the system you have invented and use your imagination further to restrict your analysis to behavior that fits the system. Oh, by the way, what's your astrological sign? Or your Chinese year? Or your Jungian archetype? Or your ethnic origin? Or your Ayurvedic body type? Or your Enneagram number? Or your age?

An experience with analysis. Even though it starts with imagination, analysis can be useful.

> 1. Divide your behavior into good behavior and bad behavior. You will have to invent or imagine a means of determining which is which.
>
> 2. Analyze the amount of time devoted to each type of behavior during a typical day.
>
> 3. Imagine what that means, or what you can do with that information.

Planning. When you plan anything, whether a speech, a party, or a spiritual revolution, the role of imagination is obvious. First you imagine what you want, and then you imagine the steps or the actions it will take to get it. Writing a plan down does not make the plan more real. The writing (or drawing) is just a representation of the plan. The plan itself is still in your head until you execute it. While you are executing it, the plan is in your perception. Then it becomes a memory and is available for recall.

One of the most useful types of planning for your personal development is called rehearsal. In this kind of planning, you imagine doing something as vividly as you can, using all your senses. This helps to establish memory patterns that can come into play when you encounter the event you are planning for. You can do this as a purely mental activity, of course, knowing that your body will be involved automatically to the extent that your imagined sensory experience is vivid enough, but the memory patterns are more easily accessed when you involve your body physically in the rehearsal, even in a small way.

During certain periods of my life I was an amateur actor in different groups. Sometimes we would have to use a small room to rehearse our play in because the theater wasn't available. Using vivid imagination we had to make three steps represent ten steps, and often we had to react physically to imagined props and furniture. At the same time, we had to keep in mind our imagined audience, so that we could maintain our proper position in relation to it. At other times, we would rehearse in one type of location only to discover that the final location for the play was completely different. That taught us flexibility, because plans, being imaginary events, don't always work out the same as the event itself.

Another thing that taught us flexibility was the fact that not everyone would remember the plan when it came time to execute it. Usually this took the form of someone forgetting their lines, not responding to a cue, or misinterpreting a cue.

As a member of the Dakar Dramatic Society in Senegal I was in a play one time called "Hello Out There," by William Saroyan, about a young man traveling through West Texas who was framed for a crime he didn't commit and was put in jail. I played the young man, and friends from the American, British, and Canadian embassies played the other characters. On the particular evening I'm writing about the little dinner theater where we put on our shorter plays was filled with men and women who were actually from West Texas. They were part of an oil exploration team, and some of them had never been to a play before, so they were somewhat rowdy and talkative during the performance.

Near the middle of the play was my big moment, a long monologue during which I would be the only one on the stage speaking. Before that could happen, however, one of the characters, my secretary in real life, was supposed to come up to my cell door and tell me that she was going to go out and see if anyone else was in the jailhouse. That would leave me alone to give my speech. Unfortunately, the rowdy audience had shaken her confidence and she gave me the line that was supposed to come after she came back when I had finished my stellar performance.

"There's no one there," she said.

I wasn't about to give up my monologue, so I said, "Go and see anyway."

"But there's no one there," she said again.

This went on for a couple more times, and finally I reached through the bars, grabbed her by the shoulders, and pulled her right up to my face, and said firmly, "Please, go out and check again! Right now!" An additional little shake brought her memory back. She left like a good girl and the stage was mine.

We can learn several useful things from this. First, thanks to rehearsal we both knew what to do when the event was in progress. My secretary needed a little reminding, but once back on track she followed the rehearsed pattern of behavior. Second, plans don't happen automatically, they happen because people carry them out. It was my motivation to complete my part of the plan that made the play successful. Without that, the play, the plan, would have fallen apart. Third, no plan is perfect, because no plan can foresee everything that might happen. This means that the purpose of the plan is more important than the plan itself. If you remember that, it makes it easier for you to change your plan as needed.

Plans have no special power. They are not sacred in any way. They are pure imagination until human beings act to make them happen, and even then a plan ought never to take precedence over the people carrying it out. People don't fail. Plans fail. And plans can be changed.

That said, plans, and rehearsal for plans can be extremely useful for giving a sense of security to your body and confidence to your mind. We'll make use of them in various parts of this book, but for now let's try something simple.

An experience with rehearsal. This will help you to get used to the process.

> 1. Think of something you need to do or want to do with someone else. It could be taking someone out for dinner, discussing finances, asking for a favor, anything.
>
> 2. In your mind, imagine doing it as clearly and as vividly as you can.
>
> 3. When you actually do it, pay close attention to how your body feels or reacts and how your mind operates while you are doing it.

Fantasy. This is what many people think imagination is, because they have been taught that "imagined" is the same as "unreal." You may think it odd, but I agree with that. Everything we think is unreal, but only if we define "reality" as information received by our mind through our sensory organs. Based on what we know about our senses, though, that definition is rather humorous. It means that "reality" is a bunch of electrical signals, processed in some mysterious way by our brain so that they are perceived by our mind as sights, sounds, touch, etc.

Hold on a minute. If I continue in that way then I'll find myself forced to assert that everything we experience is a fantasy, and I'd rather not do that right now.

Let's start over and talk about fantasy as being "unreal" experience. Let's go even further and define fantasy as "imagined experience that is improbable, highly unlikely, or totally unrelated to ordinary sensory experience." Imagining yourself as Superman, Wonder Woman, or Emperor/Empress of the world would fall into that category, as would a great many other imagined experiences.

Besides being a wonderful resource for novels, movies,

and a multitude of emotionally satisfying adventures, fantasy also has a very practical personal use.

I've already told you how your body responds to your thoughts, all your thoughts. When you imagine a sensory experience, all the muscles and nerves that would be activated by an equivalent ordinary sensory experience are activated by the imagined experience, too. Where fantasy is concerned, what this means is that if you fantasize yourself as a superhero, your body immediately starts to modify your muscles, your nerve impulses, and your internal chemistry in ways designed to simulate your fantasy image as closely as possible. The degree of modification depends entirely upon the degree of intensity and vividness you are able to conjure up, plus any inhibitions or restrictions imposed by your remembered rules, and the actual physical capabilities of your body. At the very least, such a fantasy would result in a certain amount of increase in muscle strength and sensory potential, but how much for a particular individual is anybody's guess. Still, it's a cheap workout. No kidding, though, the difference will often be measurable with equipment designed to test muscle strength and sensory perception. One brief fantasy episode may not be enough to register, of course, but with practice you can improve the effect.

No matter how wild or even abstract your fantasy is, your body will try it's best to respond in an equivalent way. Fantasy can improve your looks, or at least your appeal, and can help to create the kind of personality other people would enjoy being around.

The most powerful experience I ever had with this took place during a workshop I attended that was given by someone else. The format of the workshop was very simple. There were a few over-long relaxation meditations, and then each student in turn had an opportunity to stand on a stage and talk about himself or herself. The facilitator, who was very good and compassionate, would add helpful questions or suggestions. The powerful experience came when a young woman, perhaps eighteen or twenty years old, got up to speak. She was blonde and shy and her looks were plain, the kind of face you might not even notice in a crowd. As her shyness and low self esteem became more evident, the facilitator suggested that she repeat the statement, "I am beautiful." She needed some coaxing and everyone felt sorry for her... at first. You can't make a statement like that over and over again, even if you believe it isn't true, without fantasy being stimulated to some degree. The facilitator kept her doing it for about five minutes when suddenly there was a gasp from the audience, especially the men and including me. In my perception, it was as if a wave of some kind passed over her face, and then she was beautiful. That's right, she went from plain to beautiful in five minutes and she was besieged by men asking her for a date for the rest of the workshop.

The thing is, you don't want to live your whole life in a fantasy world that other people don't share, because that could get you into trouble. The healthy approach is to use fantasy to enhance your relationships in the same world that everyone else shares. Use your fantasies to help you feel better, and check the effects on your relationships. Then you can use that information to modify your fantasies.

An experiment with fantasy. We're going to start with something simple.

> 1. Imagine yourself taller, slimmer, stronger, or more confident than you are right now. Make it as vivid as you can. Base it on a super-hero, athlete, or actor if you want to.
>
> 2. Do your best to feel the change, and keep it up for one minute at least.
>
> 3. Next time you are with people, recall the fantasy and the feeling briefly, and notice if anyone else no-

tices anything different.

4. Repeat this daily, or several times a day, for a week, and pay attention to how often your imagination pulls you into a different state.

Self Esteem

Self esteem is a product of perception, recall, and imagination, because it depends entirely on how you perceive yourself, what you recall about yourself, and what you imagine about yourself. It is also the mental framework on which all other personal qualities are built. Confidence, for instance, is based on authority, but authority is based on the esteem in which someone or something is held. Without that esteem no authority is granted. If you want to develop your own inner authority, you have to increase your self confidence, and in order to increase your self confidence, you have to increase your self esteem, the imagined value that you give to yourself. And another good reason for increasing your self esteem is that this has a direct effect on how others value you, too.

Self esteem is almost as vital to effective relationships as the air we breathe, the water we drink and the food we eat because it is our own measure of our own value as a human being. If we think of ourselves as worthless then we open our lives to the worst kinds of exploitation. And if we do not respect ourselves there will be very few others who will respect us either. On the other hand, there are strong inhibitions in many cultures, including our modern one, of thinking well of oneself. The English terms "swelled head", "too big for your britches", "snobbish" and "you think you're better than us" are routinely applied to people who express some degree of self appreciation, and in some cultures it is considered the height of bad manners to think well of oneself. This becomes even more curious and confusing when you realize that the most successful people in any society obviously have very high self esteem, and most self help programs strongly promote good self esteem. Why does this subject include such opposing points of view?

Cultural Conflicts. Most of the cultures of the world have had strong class or caste distinctions at one time or another which have served to exalt a small minority over a much larger majority. Not only are the minority considered intrinsically better in most cases, the majority are usually considered intrinsically bad. Some people in the Hawaiian aristocracy often referred to the commoners as dirt, excrement, or other very pejorative terms.

Very typical of this common cultural pattern was the Natchez society of the lower Mississippi Valley in the central United States. Considered as a last remnant of the ancient mound-building culture of North America, it was described by French explorers in the seventeenth century. At the top of the social pyramid was a ruler with absolute power, the Great Sun. Just below him were his relatives, the Lesser Suns. Then came a class of nobles, a class of lesser nobles or honored ones, and finally the mass of commoners who were contemptuously called "Stinkards." This pattern will have a familiar ring to it all over the world.

At some point in the development of a society it makes sense to have divisions of labor, including the mental/emotional labor of leadership and administration. But that kind of labor is so important and the ones who are really good at it are so few that social value often gets mixed up with individual value. And the leaders, in addition to being better leaders, become thought of as better people. A real problem arises when the non-leaders as a group become thought of as lesser people and talented individuals born into that group later on find it difficult, dangerous, and perhaps impossible to move out of the group and use their abilities.

What does this have to do with self esteem today? The

cultural legacy of class distinctions that most of us have received from our ancestors still lingers on in overt and subtle ways. Even in an "enlightened" society like that of the modern Western nations there is a strong ongoing tendency to endow the entitled, the wealthy, the educated and, to some degree, the exceptionally talented with superior qualities as individuals, regardless of their behavior, and to endow all others not so privileged as inferior individuals, again regardless of their behavior.

Like it or not we still find that these attitudes are very common in regard to the contrasting groups of rich and famous/poor and unknown; white collar and blue collar workers; college-educated and those who are not; and, of course, racial groups. Also, the remembered dangers of competing against your "betters" are still hanging around. I can remember my Italian mother saying to me once a very long time ago when I was planning my way to fame and fortune, "Be careful you don't make the gods jealous." The "gods" don't always refer to heavenly beings: they can also be a symbol of those with political and economic power.

Because high self esteem is associated with standing out from the crowd, and standing out carries with it cultural memories of danger from jealous rulers, children today are often given subtle but pervasive hints to blend in, to not rock the boat, to refrain from doing anything that would bring too much attention to oneself. Of course there are exceptional people who do outstanding things without regard to the opinion of others about them, but what makes them so fascinating as items for gossip and storytelling is that they are exceptional.

However, high self esteem is not the problem and it wouldn't be so important were it not for the fact that excessively low self esteem is so prevalent. For it is low self esteem —a sense of unworthiness and disrespect for oneself—that reduces our ability to stand up for our rights when we are being exploited, cheated or abused; to say "NO" when it is in our best interests to do so; and to pursue the development of good relationships.

Religious Inhibitions. In the interest of helping people to be more flexible and open to spiritual influence, major Western and Eastern religions have tended to emphasize the virtue of humility and the sin of pride. While individual leaders may have used those teachings for their own ends from time to time, the overall concepts of having enough humility to realize that you yourself may not have all the answers and resources for solving life's problems, and of not having so much pride that you think you are really inherently better than everyone else, can be healthy ideas to have. These essentially good ideas, unfortunately, have frequently become distorted in practice.

Humility is false, for instance, when you are suppressing the talents and abilities that are natural to you for the sake of getting approval from another human being. If you do that you will be living a lie that will take its physical, emotional and mental toll on you. That kind of humility is neither spiritual nor beneficial to you or to your community.

Pride, on the other hand, is not sinful when it is an honest recognition of who you are and what you can do. But some people have come to believe so strongly that any form of self recognition is bad, they go out of their way to squelch all appreciation of anyone's goodness, especially that of themselves and of their family. In what is perhaps a well-intentioned effort, many not only suppress the recognition of goodness and improvement, they negate it most thoroughly with that all-time destroyer of self esteem: the terrible social weapon of criticism.

Nevertheless, if you stop to think about it you will understand that true pride and true humility are one and the same. Each one involves an honest appraisal of your state as a human being and your place in the world. If you think that is a good state and a good place, you have a healthy self esteem. If you think it is a bad state or a bad place, but you can learn how to change it, then you can develop a healthy self esteem. If you think the state and the place are bad and you don't deserve any better, your low self esteem will always get in the way of your happiness and success.

More on self criticism. When I was in high school I loved science and I liked my science teacher, but I was bored by the way it was taught and slacked off on my homework. The teacher, apparently trying out some sort of student psychology he must have learned began criticizing me in class for all sorts of things in the vain hope that this would spur me on to greater effort. However, my reaction was to move away from the criticism instead, and I took to spending the science hour in the local pool hall. I got pretty good at pool, but I graduated high school with a D- average, number 64 in a class of 65.

I can't blame my science teacher for that, nor any of the other teachers who used criticism as a teaching method. I rebelled and withdrew because my own self criticism was so heavy I couldn't handle any more. They were doing what they'd been taught to do, but my reactions were my own.

Parents are the next easy target to lay blame on. Maybe my self criticism came from their criticism of me. Well, my father was pretty critical in my opinion, although far less critical than his father was to him. My mother's criticism was more subtle: she was always telling me how much potential I had, and I interpreted that to mean I wasn't okay the way I was. Still, they were just trying to help me become a better person and to do better in school. I was the one who took it so personally,

So, was it my fault? No, I wasn't to blame either because

I didn't know how to react any differently. I had no model, or guideline, or training for dealing with criticism in a more positive way.

Was it society's fault? No, because "society" does not really exist as an independent being with the power of self-aware action. It is only an artificial idea that we use to talk about a bunch of people who share certain kinds of behavior and boundaries. Society can't be at fault for anything.

It wasn't anyone's fault. The whole process of finding fault is based on the practice of looking for what is wrong so we can fix it. That's not bad for working on machines, but it is extremely inefficient when working on human beings. The most efficient way to change human behavior, including your own, is to reinforce what's right, instead of trying to fix what's wrong. Criticism, however well meant, has the opposite effect because it is based on fear, rather than love. The desire for approval is one of the strongest of all human motivations. The loss of approval is one of our greatest fears. This is why criticism has such power; it is an expression of disapproval. It is bad enough when someone you care for or need disapproves of you in some way, but it is literally disabling when you disapprove of yourself. You can always move away from someone else's influence, or change your behavior to please them (well, maybe not always), but if you disapprove of yourself you are stuck because you can't get away and even changing behavior may not work. I recall the story of a man who smoked for thirty years and finally gave it up because his church said it was sinful, but he felt continually guilty and unhappy because he could not forgive himself for having done something so bad for so long.

The worst criticism of all is self criticism. Especially if it is based on the idea that you are no good no matter what. If this is your problem only you can make the decision and start the practice of thinking differently about yourself. And if you know someone else who is highly self critical whom you want to help, only they can make the same decision. One of the most frustrating things you can do is to try and convince someone that they are good when they don't think so. It's like trying to give someone a piece of cake through a screen. It can be seen as good, smelled as good, but it just doesn't reach them. They've got to make their own cake and eat it before the screen can come down and they can share cake with you.

Self criticism has some positive benefits, surprisingly. In some cases it can make you so angry with yourself that you begin to make changes. And it's a fairly effective technique for avoiding risk. If you criticize yourself just the right amount in just the right way you can convince yourself that you don't have the talent, skill, nerve or right to try something new (and possibly make a fool of yourself). So it can be used to avoid a potential loss of approval, self- or otherwise. But these benefits cannot make up for the havoc it wreaks on your life when it becomes a habit.

We can all live with occasional self criticism, even if we would be better off without it. But habitual self criticism is devastating. First, it makes it practically impossible to ever feel good about anything you do, since you will automatically put yourself down as soon as good feelings begin. Suppose you were a person with an HSC (habitual self criticism) syndrome. If you won an Oscar for acting, one of the highest professional awards, you would probably feel an initial flush of pleasure at the announcement, but then you would find fault with the way you were dressed, the way you walked up to the podium, the way you said thank you, the way you returned, and no doubt your performance as well. In a very short time the thrill of recognition will have turned to ashes. People who are habitual self criticizers rarely enjoy anything for very long.

Self criticism interferes with developing talents and skills. It is commonly assumed that self criticism will help to improve our behavior and increase our level of achievement, but just the contrary is true if the self criticism becomes habitual. We learn better and faster by reward rather than by punishment. As I already mentioned, babies learn to walk and to speak by focusing on what they do right and repeating it, not by remembering what they do wrong and avoiding it. The greater the reward we get for each correct action, that is, the more completely a felt need is satisfied, the more eagerly we repeat the action and thereby improve our skill. But the greater the punishment for any action—and all criticism is felt as punishment—the more we avoid the action as much as we can. If the positive benefit of an action is great enough we will persist in doing it in spite of criticism. The whole process of improvement is much harder, however, because at the same time we will be subconsciously avoiding or resisting the action, too. Constant self criticism makes everything we do much more difficult because of that.

Self criticism diminishes the quality of our relationships. The more critical you are with yourself, the more critical you will tend to be with others, and the more critical they will tend to be of you. The habit of inner-directed criticism easily extends outward. People with good self esteem do not enjoy being around highly self critical people, not only because it's unpleasant in itself, but because the can sense themselves being criticized, consciously or subconsciously, as well. Criticism is not just verbal, you see. It can be perceived in all the ways you react in facial expression and body movement to who and what is happening around you. So the result is that you are usually left with other highly self critical people and you all just reinforce each other's behavior.

The pain of perfection. To be perfect seems like such a good ideal. It also happens to be a warrior-type obsession, but even if it weren't, it still sounds good. To be faultless, without flaw, untarnished and pure ... how wonderful!

The real problems that arise from pursuing that ideal do not come from the ideal itself, but from the interpretation of what perfection means.

To be faultless implies that there is some standard to go by. But where does that standard come from? The Ten Commandments? The Eight-fold Path of Buddha? The Laws of the Koran? Family values? Society's laws? A teacher's rules? Your own decisions about right and wrong? Are you perfect if you follow one set of guidelines and not another? For instance, are you perfect if you follow all of your father's rules of behavior and not your mother's. Or vice-versa? And if you fail to meet the standard you accept, what does that mean? Can you redeem yourself by "correcting" your behavior, or are you forever condemned because you slipped however many times? I'm not providing answers here; I'm raising questions for you to think about. You have a right to follow any standard you choose, and to determine whether not meeting that standard means you are faulty (it could also mean you just didn't meet the standard). What I want to point out is that if your standards aren't clear and consistent, then your feelings about yourself, and your attitudes about yourself, and your behavior toward yourself won't be clear or consistent, either.

What is a flaw? Some people believe that all humans are flawed. If so, then as long as you are human you are going to be imperfect and it makes more sense to accept that than to fight it and feel bad about it for the rest of your life. Some people believe that so-called character or physical "defects" are signs of flaws in a person. This, however, gets us into standards again because what is a defect to one person may be a positive attribute to another. In the laboratory, for instance, it is possible to make sapphires that are totally free from physical defects and consistent in color and quality. But the most valuable sapphires are ones that are dug out of the earth and polished, and that have certain visible flaws. Their value comes from their imperfection. In a sense, then, the most perfect sapphire has to be imperfect.

Abraham Lincoln was full of defects according to detractors during his terms in office. He was called, among other things, "a wet rag," "a weakling," and "the root of evil." Even his Gettysburg Address was described by the Chicago Times as "silly, flat, and dishwatery." Physically, he was perceived by some as awkward, ungainly, and ugly. But his physical presence was still impressive and it was his character that led our nation into a new era. Was he perfect? It all depends on what you consider as flaws.

Along the same lines it is interesting to note that a garden with weeds is considered flawed, yet a weed is just a plant growing where we don't think it should. A flowering plant called lantana is carefully cultivated in California as an ornamental, but in Hawaii it is a weed wildly overtaking native plants. Qualities that qualify you as flawed in one part of the world or in one period of your life may make you perfect in another. Intellectuals may be unfit for the gym, but successful in the laboratory; athletes may stumble in the library, but excel in the arena. What is a flaw?

Untarnished is generally used to mean polished so that the true nature can shine clearly, or uncontaminated by contact with something that might lower its value. Untarnished makes us think of shiny metal, like gold, silver, and brass, or people with unsullied reputations who have never done what some would call wrong. Again, it sure sounds good. Realistically, though, polished metals can be useful as well as beautiful, but so can tarnished ones. The green patina of bronze, for instance, is a desirable condition that enhances its beauty. And anodized aluminum is purposely tarnished to protect and beautify it. With people, the "tarnish" gives them experience that can be extremely valuable in teaching or helping others. Think of such groups as Alcoholics Anonymous and the prisoners who teach young people how not to go to prison. Sometimes the person with the perfectly untarnished reputation is the most imperfect one for the job.

How about being pure? Now that is really a loaded concept. Take the idea of racial purity, for example. There isn't any such animal. Everyone has a mixed heritage and it doesn't take much research to find it out. Some people decide on their own that certain racial mixtures aren't good, but that's just a made-up rule that you don't find any justification for in nature. It used to be fairly common and it is still fairly current to think of purity in terms of sexual conduct. Sexual fantasies are called impure thoughts, and sexual behaviors that don't follow some group's arbitrary rules are called impure acts. People who have engaged in such thoughts or acts are said to have polluted themselves and must be cleansed. I don't have any interest in what your particular rules for sexual conduct are, but I am interested in clear thinking and speaking. If you want to define certain behavior as pure and other behavior as impure, and decide that certain acts are polluting and other acts are cleansing, then go ahead and enjoy (or dread) the consequences. Just remember that the decisions are yours and no one else's. Even if you think the rules came from a perfect source, it's your decision to follow them or not to follow them.

The whole idea of purity as an ideal comes from the assumption that the more sameness there is the better. Yet, we don't find this at all in the world around us. Absolutely pure water—distilled water—is man-made and it is dead water. To nourish us it needs minerals, flora and fauna, H_2O_2, and electrical charges. Then it is living water. The beauty of an amethyst comes from iron impurities that turn the quartz purple. All of our basic foods, even the organically-grown and pesticide-free ones, are hybrids. All work and no play make Jack a dull boy and variety is the spice of life.

The ideal of perfection may also give rise to an attempt to reach an unchanging, "perfect" state of mind, body or circumstance. In this case, once a state is reached which is defined as perfect, then any change in that state must represent imperfection. If a perfect day is thought of as a bright sun shining in a clear blue sky, then a single cloud would "mar" that perfection, even though it would be a natural event. If a perfect body is supposed to look like the model in the magazine and yours doesn't, then yours is obviously imperfect. If a perfect mind is supposed to think only good thoughts and you happen to be upset for a moment because your soul-mate didn't take out the garbage, then your mind is imperfect.

Ideals are good to have, but when anything less than the ideal is called bad, trouble is on the way. More specifically, if you think of yourself as bad whenever you are imperfect (according to your own ideals), then you are in for a whole lot of unhappiness and failure because the idea of perfection as an unchanging state holds a deadly trap. The trap is hidden in the assumption that any state of mind, body or circumstance can be unchanging.

If you actually allow yourself to observe and study yourself and the world around you, it will soon be clear that nothing ever remains the same—not stars, mountains, seasons, events, people, and certainly not you. Now, you can fault yourself for every time your internal or external behavior doesn't match your ideal and thereby cause yourself to frequently suffer from low self esteem, or you can applaud the changes you like, tolerate the ones you don't, and treat perfection as a journey rather than as a place to be.

It is one thing to understand low self esteem and why you might have it, and quite another to do something about it. Here are some ways and means that work.

Seven techniques for self esteem. These techniques can be done as a seven-minute exercise, spending one minute on each one in turn; or individually whenever you think they are appropriate.

I Am What I Am. This was a favorite saying of the cartoon character, Popeye. He would also, from time to time, let everyone within hearing distance know in no uncertain terms that he was a "sailor man." He clearly defined himself, particularly after every success, to reinforce his sense of self esteem, and you can do the same. The world is what you think it is, and you are what you think you are. To raise your self esteem and increase your effectiveness, define yourself—honestly—in the most positive way you can. You do this by saying to yourself, aloud or silently, "I am ..." and adding any positive quality, attribute, talent or skill that you can remember. Of course, if you are like a lot of other people, it could be much easier at first to come up with negative definitions like "I am lazy" or "I am not very good at cleaning house", but do your best to ignore those during this technique. The negatives may exist, but they're not important right now and you can do something about them later if you want to. For the moment concentrate on positive things. Here are some examples just to help you get started. Yours may be completely different:

1. "I am alive."
2. "I am a mother/father" (you can add "good" if you believe it).
3. "I am a loyal friend."
4. "I am a good worker."
5. "I am healthy."
6. "I am a ..." (add your profession, like secretary or sailor man).

Keep repeating your self definitions for at least one minute. If you can only think of a few at first, just keep repeating them for the whole minute. It may be helpful to write them down, but change or add to the list whenever you want.

Remember When. One of the things that keep low self esteem alive is the habit of frequently recalling your mistakes. In this technique the purpose is to help counteract the effect of that by purposely recalling situations in which you did something right. Notice that I said, "right", not "perfect." It is always possible for anything to have been done better than it was. The point here is not to review what you could have improved on, but to honor yourself for whatever you did that worked, even a little bit. Here are some examples taken from my life:

1. The time I first jumped out of a tree.
2. The time I got my driver's license.
3. The time I got an "A" grade on my term paper.
4. The time I won at poker.
5. The time I didn't lose my temper when my son rolled my Mustang.

They don't have to be big events. Even recalling very small successes will leave you feeling better about yourself. During the minute or more you dwell on these memories, let yourself remember how good you felt at the time, too.

Wannabee. A "wannabee" is a person who "wants to be," wants to look and/or act like, someone else who is admired. There are Elvis wannabees, Marilyn Monroe wannabees, Arnold Schwarzenegger wannabees, Madonna wannabees, and as many others as there are people who symbolize success. Often wannabees are put down, as if there were something wrong with wanting to be like someone else who already has something you want. You may have been criticized already at some point in your life for dressing or acting like someone else and told to "be yourself." What the critic usually means is, "don't be anything except what I want you to be."

"Be yourself" doesn't have any meaning if you aren't clear

about who you are, and "be yourself" can be the worst thing to do if your behavior and habits are mostly negative. Some people, when faced with this problem, go off somewhere to "find themselves," but the main benefit of that is to get away from the critic. You aren't elsewhere. You are right where you are. Most of what you are, however, is an accumulation of learned attitudes, habits and behaviors. That's right, "You" are mostly what you have learned to be, and you learned it from someone else. You have your own uniqueness, naturally, but your unique self is like the material on which a portrait is painted. The artist represents the people you learn from, the paint is experience, and the material is you. The same artist using the same paint will produce different effects on canvas, rice paper, cardboard or silk. All of us learn from the people around us, even when we aren't aware of it, and even when what we learn isn't what we want. I recall vividly an occasion about twenty years ago when I was very angry at one of my sons and I had the strangest sensation for a moment that I was my father. It shook me up so much I went off by myself for a while to analyze it. I finally realized that in that moment I was matching almost exactly an anger pattern of my father's that I had incorporated subconsciously. Fortunately for my son, I immediately began practicing a more effective reaction pattern.

Since we learn attitudes and behaviors from other people anyway, we might as well make a conscious choice of what we want to learn and from whom so we can raise our self esteem. That's what the technique of Wannabee is all about. It is not to try and become another person because we don't like ourselves; it is to learn the best of what we can from another person so we can like ourselves even more.

The way to practice the Wannabee technique is to think of people who have qualities you would like to have, to decide to develop those qualities in yourself, and then to practice those qualities in your thinking, feeling and actions by using the other person as your "teacher." You can pick different qualities from different people, and these people might be living or non-living, real or fiction, famous or local. You could choose the dedication of Mother Theresa, the enthusiasm of your best friend, the poise of Princess Leia (from Star Wars), and the persistence of Mahatma Gandhi. Or anything else you want. The thing to keep in mind is that you are practicing these things to make them your own.

Posturetalk. The way you hold your body not only tells other people a lot about how you think of yourself, it actually affects how you think about yourself. Try this experiment:

> 1. While sitting in a chair, let your head fall forward, cross your arms, then bring one hand up and slightly pull your lower lip out with your thumb and forefinger. After 15 seconds,
>
> 2. Take your hand away and uncross your arms, lift your head and look forward, and place your hands flat on top of your thighs. Hold this position for 15 seconds.
>
> 3. How did you feel in each position, and what did you think of? How were they different?

If you were like most people you would have felt a bit depressed or uncertain in the first position, and a bit more hopeful or certain in the second. Even if your postural patterns for these reactions are different, it is easy to discover the relationship between posture, feelings and thoughts.

The Posturetalk technique is a way of getting your body to "speak" to your mind and emotions and help them to create better self esteem. To do it you explore different ways of sitting, standing, walking, moving and positioning your arms and hands, until you find several postures that help you think and feel better. Then you practice those until you can do them well whenever you want to. As an alternative, you can remember times when you were at your best and reproduce the postures you held then. I do this sometimes by remembering my best days as a Marine Corps sergeant. Another alternative is to practice the postures used by other people who seem to have good self esteem.

Saturation Praise. The best antidote to self criticism is self praise. Wait! Before you back off, I mean deserved praise. To put it another way, you can counteract the esteem-lowering effects of criticism with compliments based on real experience. Such compliments reinforce your self respect by reminding you that you're not all bad, even if you're not as perfect as you'd like to be. To be effective as esteem builders and criticism healers, though, the compliments have to be true. They do not, however, have to be world-shaking. Acknowledging anything in the least bit worthwhile is very useful.

To do the technique of Saturation Praise you spend a full minute or more giving yourself as many compliments as you can think of without allowing any pauses for rebuttal. If you can't think of enough to fill a minute at first, then you keep repeating what you have. Some examples to get you started:

1. I have a nice smile.
2. My skin is clear.
3. My handwriting is legible.
4. I make good brownies.
5. My friends can always count on me.
6. I never hit little old ladies (unless they hit me first),
7. or whatever suits your life and behavior.

When you do this as directed for a full minute you will usually feel a lot better. It is very important to realize that even a justified criticism does not negate the reality and importance of a justified compliment.

Giving Up Guilt. The way to give up guilt is to change

your mind about what you did or didn't do. I don't mean to pretend it didn't happen; I mean to change your mind about what it means. This is called self forgiveness.

Other people can forgive you all they want, but it is what you think about yourself that really matters, and if you don't forgive yourself as a result of their forgiveness, then what they think or do doesn't matter. Even God can forgive you, but if you don't forgive yourself you will still feel guilty. So what's a person to do?

Use the Giving Up Guilt Technique. This technique is very simple and effective if you do it on a regular basis.

> 1. Imagine a black file cabinet, two-drawer or four-drawer, it's up to you. Inside this cabinet, representing one area of your memory, are filed away all the things you feel guilty about.
>
> 2. Consciously think of an incident and pull out a file to symbolize it. The file might contain sounds of things said or unsaid, or pictures of things done or undone.
>
> 3. Listen and look and then decide if you can do anything about it now. If you can do something, decide to do it, put a little red "active" sticker on the file and put it back in the cabinet.
>
> 4. If there is nothing you can do about it now, you may as well forgive yourself (remembering that forgiveness is not approval), so imagine you have a large rubber stamp and stamp "FORGIVEN" on the file and put it in a white file cabinet representing another area of your memory. You can pull it out again and feel guilty about it whenever you want, but that's just self indulgence.
>
> 5. Do this with detailed imagination and you will truly feel differently about the incident and about yourself. The more often you do it the better you will

feel. If there is a really major event you feel guilty about, break it up into smaller segments and work on one piece at a time as you feel ready. You can change the colors of the file cabinets, too, if you wish.

Dogooder. Self esteem comes from how we think about ourselves, and how we think about ourselves comes at least partly from a self-assessment of our own actions and non-actions. The previous technique dealt with the past; this one deals with the future.

Dogooder is just a name for the esteem-building practice of doing something good for someone else, preferably without caring about the credit. You do it because it's good, and you're good because you do it. It doesn't matter if anyone else knows about it. A hard but effective way to practice this is to do small favors for relatives and friends without them asking and perhaps without them being aware of what you've done. Here are some ideas:

1. Making beds for someone else.
2. Doing dishes without waiting to be asked.
3. Washing cars or windows for someone.
4. Picking up litter in public places.
5. Filling the gas tank when you borrow a car.
6. Doing someone else's chores.
7. Sharing your favorite treats.

The hard part of this practice is doing these favors for people you know without it being openly appreciated. If you find it too hard, that is, if it's too painful for you not to get credit, then you'd better not do it in the first place.

An easier form of Dogooder that will still help you feel good about yourself is helping others who are really in need. Here are just a few ideas. If you pay attention, there will undoubtedly be many more opportunities in your community.:

1. Volunteering for a non-profit agency.
2. Supporting ecology groups.

3. Donating to animal shelters or charities that help people.

Self esteem affects every part of your life. If it's low, your life suffers; if it's good, life is more enjoyable and your relationships are more effective. If you dare to make it high, your performance and your happiness soar out of sight.

CHAPTER SIX
YOUR RELATIONSHIP WITH YOUR SPIRIT

This chapter is probably not at all what you thought it was going to be. That's because, in English, the word "spirit" has so many different meanings.

The most fundamental meaning of the word is "essence." That's all well and good, but there are many ways to think of the essence of something. For some people, "spirit" refers to the essence of alcoholic beverages, produced by a process of distillation. This kind of spirit includes brandy, vodka, gin, etc. However, this chapter is not about alcohol.

For other people, "spirit" refers to non-physical entities that inhabit material things, like nature spirits, or to entities that used be physical, like the spirits or the dead, or to things that represent the essence of something abstract, like the spirit of a civilization, or to angels and immortal beings vast in scope and beyond our understanding. I'm not going to talk about any of them here, either.

For still other people, the essence of a human being is a mysterious something called the "soul." This chapter is not about your soul in the way that most people think about it.

What I am going to talk about, and provide demonstrations and techniques for, relates to your spirit in terms of energy, and what that has to do with your relationships in general.

Your Physical Energy

I have already talked just a little about some of your physical energy when I described how your body transforms sensory information from the world around you into electrical impulses that travel along your nervous system. Now I will go much more in depth with this subject.

Without sufficient physical energy you can't kiss a lover, hug a friend, or run away from an enemy. Most people don't give much thought to their physical energy, taking it for granted that they either have it or they don't. In fact, a truly amazing number of people have the idea that energy is some kind of physical substance you have inside you that can be poured in or drained out. What's even worse is that there are some people who honestly believe that other people can suck out their energy, leaving them depleted and sick. In order to get rid of such fears and enable you to have as much energy as you want to for your relationships, I'm going to take some time to fill you in on how your physical energy system really works.

Cell Energy. Operating muscles, extracting wastes, making new cells, healing wounds, and using your brain are constant, everyday activities that require energy. It's fairly obvious that the food we eat, the water we drink, and the air we breathe all have something to do with our energy. They do, of course, but only indirectly.

The most direct source of all the energy needed by our living cells comes from the molecules of a chemical compound called Adenosine Triphosphate (ATP), which is created inside our cells. When your body needs energy to do something, the ATP molecules are broken apart and the energy released by that (the electron waves) are then used for the body's various activities. However, it takes a lot of energy to make the ATP molecules, so where does that energy come from? Here's where the water, the air, and the food come in.

The water you drink provides the environment, and some of the nutrients, in which the chemical and energetic activity of the body can take place. Water itself is a highly energetic substance, constantly breaking itself down and reforming, so it's not impossible that it is also a source of energy for the body, but no one as yet has done any well-known studies along those lines.

Food is the major fuel source for the body, without a doubt. However, whether you go out for dinner with someone and eat a meal of pork roast, potatoes, and cabbage with chocolate fudge and ice cream for dessert; or whether your dinner consists of a green salad topped with oil and vinegar and lean chicken with an apple for dessert, your body breaks it all down into sugars and fats and high-energy-potential molecules derived from them. These sugar molecules have a lot of energy, but the fat molecules have twice as much. Muscles prefer the fat energy, and the brain and nerve cells can only use the sugar energy. Both the sugar and fat molecules are broken apart inside the cells to release energy for the creation of ATP.

Oxygen from the air plays a vital role in this energy release. Some cells can make ATP without it, but the presence of oxygen in the cells can increase production by eighteen times.

All of this energetic activity produces three side effects: waste products, primarily carbon dioxide and water, most of which is expelled when you exhale; excess fat, most of which is stored where you don't want it; and another form of energy called heat.

Heat energy. Healthy human beings maintain an almost constant body temperature of 37 degrees Celsius, or 98.6 degrees Fahrenheit, although the highest body temperature ever recorded in a healthy person was that of a marathon runner just after a race. His temperature at that moment was 41 degrees Celsius, or 105.8 Fahrenheit, high enough for hospitalization in normal circumstances. Ordinarily, our body is very sensitive to internal and external temperature changes, and our perception is sensitive enough to tell us when a lover is in the right mood or a child needs care and attention.

Most people take body heat for granted, unless the temperature goes too far one way or the other, but most of that heat is a by-product of all the molecular activity going on in the cells. Some of our body heat also comes from our surroundings, when the environmental temperature is higher than our body surface temperature, even just a little bit.

To maintain its healthy state, the body has to give off excess heat into the environment. It does this mainly by radiation and evaporation (perspiration), although exhaling also plays a role. Certain kinds of mental activity, like meditation or concentration, can stimulate the production of excess heat that the body has to get rid of. When I hold meetings in the summer and there is a group of about twenty or more people their heat radiation can make the room uncomfortably hot even if we have an air conditioner. The same kinds of mental activity, with a different focus, may actually diminish the production of personal heat.

Our heat energy plays an important role in our relations with other people, because we tend to equate temperature differences with emotional differences. A person with a comfortably warm envelope of air around his or her body is generally considered emotionally warm and pleasant to be with. If the envelope is uncomfortably warm, we feel uncomfortable around that person and the tendency is to interpret excessive warmth as suppressed anger, which it sometimes is. If we perceive that the person's air envelope is comfortably cool, the tendency is to interpret the coolness as signifying that the person is more intellectual than emotional, or perhaps a very calm type of person. If the personal envelope is uncomfortably cool, the interpretation may be that he or she is emotionally aloof or distant. In English we might call such a person a "cold fish." Sometimes these interpretations are invalid, because there may be purely physiological or mental reasons for the temperature differences. Sometimes, however, emotions really may be involved, and we'll cover that later.

Muscular Energy. Although all muscular activity involves cell energy and heat energy, in this section I'm going to talk about the use of muscles for movement, posture, and resistance.

It takes energy to move our bodies around; to touch, pick up, or move things; to push; to pull; to react to people, events, and circumstances; to stand; to sit; and even to lie down. It also takes energy not to move, not to feel, and not to react. All of this involves muscular energy.

We use muscular energy to caress or hit someone, and also to not caress or hit someone. We use muscular energy to express how we feel, and to suppress how we feel. The state of our muscles has a very direct effect on the state of our relationships.

It was stated above that people can be very sensitive to the degree of heat that your body generates. The same is true for the degree of tension you have in your muscles, because this affects your movements, your postures, your skin color, and your heat radiation, all of which other people use, consciously or subconsciously, to interpret your state of mind, your feelings, and your intentions.

Basically, muscles relax and contract in response to physical or mental activity and conditions. Dehydration can cause extended contraction (or tension) and rehydration can produce relaxation. Worry can cause contraction and confidence can cause relaxation.

Generally speaking, encountering someone or something that we like tends to induce acceptance and relaxation, while encountering someone or something we don't like tends to induce resistance and tension. Interestingly, recalling or anticipating what we like or don't like will have the same effect on our body reactions.

Too much relaxation can be as bad for a relationship as too much tension. It's as hard to have a good time with a limp dishrag as it is with an iron post. However, since too much tension is much more common, it's good to have a simple way to relax the excess tension when you want to.

A simple relaxation exercise: This is another form of *piko-piko* that's useful for relaxing and calming down.

1. Sit, stand, or lie down, your choice.

2. Place one or both hands over your navel.

3. As you inhale and exhale, keep your attention on the sensation of your hand(s) against your skin. If you absolutely must do something more with your mind, just think the word, "relax" over and over.

4. Continue for at least one or two minutes, the longer the better.

Your Emotional Energy

There is no general agreement in the world on what emotions are, but there is general agreement that people experience emotions. Therefore, some of the things I will have to say about emotions may not be agreeable to everyone. Nevertheless, I will say them anyway, because these ideas have helped thousands of people to deal with emotions more effectively.

First of all, we must discard the misguided, ineffective

idea that emotions are a material substance like water, or air, or soil. Even as a metaphor that doesn't work very well for dealing with them. We don't walk around with our bodies full of emotions, we can't get rid of emotions like we get rid of toxins, and we don't "pick up" emotions from other people like we pick up germs.

Emotions are waves of energy that carry information, similar to the way that microwave energy waves carry information through the air, or electrical energy waves carry information through our nervous system. And like sound waves that travel through the air, emotional waves do not exist until something starts them waving. There is no sound until something vibrates strongly enough to create sound waves. There is no emotion until something vibrates strongly enough to create an emotional wave.

I know, I know, this probably goes against everything you've been taught about emotions. Just bear with me and keep an open mind.

You experience emotions when something vibrates. So, what vibrates? The answer is, your muscles. Emotions are energetic reactions to memories or expectations. When an event stimulates a remembrance (without conscious awareness) or a recall (with conscious awareness), and when that switches on important rules about good or bad, pleasure or pain, your muscles react in a way that sends waves of emotional energy through your body and into the world around you. Your body might react emotionally to a smell, or to a shape, or to a particular pattern or intensity of light, or something else without your mind knowing why. And, of course, your mind can react emotionally to any number of things.

An Emotional Experience. The two most important things that determine the nature of an emotional reaction are the rule or rules you have about a memory or expectation, and the degree of overall muscle tension currently in your body. Of these two, muscle tension takes precedence.

1. In any comfortable body position, relax all of your muscles as completely as you can.

2. While keeping your muscles relaxed, get very angry about something you recall or imagine.

3. If your muscles really are relaxed, you will find that you simply cannot experience anger.

4. Try the same thing with fear and you will get the same result.

5. Try the same thing with joy and you will get the same result, although you may find the state of relaxation itself to be somewhat pleasurable.

The thing to learn from this is how important your state of tension, or stress, if you prefer, is to your emotional state. Emotions of any kind require an increase in muscle tension for their existence. Naturally, any muscle activity affects your physical energy, as well. You can, quite literally, become physically exhausted from sustained emotional activity, although your endurance is greater with positive emotions.

Positive and negative emotions. Physiologically, both positive and negative emotions only exist in the presence of certain kinds of muscle tension. Negative emotions require a certain level of steadily increasing or sustained muscle tension. Too little tension and the negative emotion disappears. Too much tension and the negative emotional reaction is suppressed because the muscles cannot move and the memory that would stimulate the emotional reaction cannot be accessed. Sustained tension at this level has many unpleasant side effects, unfortunately, on your body, your mind, and your relationships. And please note that it is not the emotion that is suppressed, it is the memory or expectation of an event plus their accompanying rules that have been suppressed. Unless they are activated, emotions don't happen.

Positive emotions require steadily increasing or sustained

pulsations of muscular tension and relaxation to exist. No tension, no positive emotion. No relaxation accompanying the tension, and the emotion ceases to be positive. Positive emotions generally have beneficial side effects on your body, your mind, and your relationships.

Emotional range and intensity. In the English language there are dozens of words that describe different positive and negative emotions, but this is misleading. Actually, all human beings only experience two emotions: happiness and unhappiness. All the different words are really only describing variations in associated circumstances and intensity.

Sorrow is an unhappy feeling associated with loss; sadness is an unhappy feeling associated with regret; contentment is a happy feeling associated with a state of wholeness; cheerfulness is a happy feeling associated with free-flowing energy.

An intensification of these experiences, which means an increase in the amplitude of the energy involved, may result in a different name being given to the experience. Thus, intense sorrow may be called grief; intense sadness may be called despair; intense contentment may be called fulfillment; and intense cheerfulness may be called joy.

Nevertheless, it all comes down to happiness and unhappiness as the basic emotions being expressed.

The source of emotions. I want to make this very clear, because this is a radical idea and it is essential to good relationships: emotions are nothing more, and nothing less, than energetic reactions to your own thoughts.

Let me put it another way: emotions follow thoughts. Are you listening?

One important conclusion from this idea is that other people do not make you happy or unhappy. I apologize if this concept goes against the entire life pattern that some of you readers may use for dealing with relationships, but that's the way it is. Some people may give other people the responsibility for their happiness or blame them for their unhappiness, but that's a lie. People are happy or unhappy according to how they think about their experiences, and for no other reason.

I once attended a conference in Colorado where different teachers, including me, were giving workshops and lectures. One of the teachers was a young Frenchman whose name I do not remember, unfortunately. His topic was "How To Be Happy." I wasn't able to attend his workshop, but I did go to his lecture, and it was an effort to keep myself from laughing and crying all the way through it.

The problem was not his concept, which was excellent (meaning that I agreed with it wholeheartedly), but with the fact that so few people in the audience could understand it. Some of the dialogue during the question and answer period went like this:

Student A: "But what if my husband left me?"

Teacher: "Be happy."

Student B: "But what if I lose my job?"

Teacher: "Be happy."

Student C: "But what if I get sick?"

Teacher: "Be happy."

The teacher was sincere, but the students couldn't get it. His message was simply that happiness is a choice, and those students could not let go of the idea that people and circumstances dictate happiness.

Of course it's difficult to be happy when a marriage breaks up or a job is lost or someone gets sick. Difficult, yes, but not impossible. It's not impossible, because the feeling comes from you, not from elsewhere.

Here's how it works:

A. Someone does something.

B. Your body reminds you of the related rules.

135

C. You opt to accept the rule or change it.

D. Your body reacts emotionally according to your decision.

People generally have the most trouble with the "C" part, because they've developed a habit of accepting the current rules without question so quickly that it seems like the situation goes directly from "A" to "D" without a break and without any realization that a decision was made.

How do I know that this is the way it is? Well, it's my theory based on helping hundreds of people to change their emotional reactions in just a few moments by consciously changing their rules.

A fast technique for changing rules: In my book, Healing For The Millions, I describe a very fast way to change emotional reactions. Here is another fast, non-verbal technique called TFR (standing for Think—Feel—Relax).

> 1. Think of a situation in your life that typically produces an unhappy reaction.
>
> 2. Locate the place in your body where you feel this reaction.
>
> 3. Concentrate all of your attention on relaxing that part of your body.
>
> 4. When that part of your body feels better, think of the situation again and note any change in your reaction.
>
> 5. Repeat, if necessary, until there is no more unhappy reaction when you think of the situation.

The only problem with this technique is that some people think it is too simple to work. Well, it does work, but you have to try it.

Your Mental Energy

Every time you think a thought you cause a ripple in the fabric of the universe.

It isn't a big ripple, of course, but it doesn't have to be in order to produce a big effect. After all, when a giant tree is ready to fall the gentle touch of a finger will finish the job. Likewise, the right thought at the right time can affect the whole world.

Your thoughts have the greatest influence on your own body. Every single thought that you have will produce some degree of reaction in your cells. Some thoughts will only have an insignificant effect on a few cells, and some thoughts will stimulate radical changes in major organs and muscles.

One year I went skiing in the mountains of California when it was bitterly cold. While riding in a long chair lift my gloved hands got so cold I was afraid they would freeze. So I imagined that my hands were close to a warm campfire and I mentally repeated the words, "My hands are warm" over and over. In about five minutes my hands were toasty warm inside the gloves. The real significance of this is that in order for my hands to become warm in that environment information had to leap throughout my nervous system; a multitude of muscle cells had to relax and contract and relax to produce extra heat; veins, arteries, and capillaries had to relax; blood flow had to increase; my lymph system had to become more active; and probably even more stuff had to happen so that my hands would get warm. And all I did was think of fire and mentally repeat some words.

In some of my classes I demonstrate a phenomenon called "telekinesis," the ability to move matter with the mind. It's very simple. All I do is to ask someone in the audience to hand me a pen. Ta-da! Instant telekinesis. With the power of my mind alone, expressed in words, I have caused a pen to move from ten to fifteen feet away right into my hand. Now, that might sound like a joke, but it isn't. What I did was to use a thought to stimulate an existing behavior pattern, in this case a natural desire to be helpful on the part of someone else, in order to move an object without any effort on my part. The implication is that thoughts are most powerful when they work with existing energy patterns rather than against them.

I want to emphasize that it isn't the amount of energy in the thought itself that makes the difference, because thoughts just don't put out very much energy. The greatest effect of a thought comes from its ability to stimulate, switch on, or recall an existing behavior pattern that does produce or release a lot of energy. This happens most frequently and most powerfully when a thought relates directly to one or more rules governing the primary motivations of love, power, or harmony. In particular, when mental energy turns on emotional energy the effects can be widespread, involving local groups and even nations. I'll have more to say about this in later chapters.

Your Subtle Energy

This section may require a bit of mind-stretching for some people, because it borders on an area of knowledge usually considered esoteric. So far I have talked about your physical energy, which includes heat and other radiant energy from your body; your emotional energy, which affects your body and your mind; and your mental energy, which affects your emotions and your body. Now it's time to bring up your subtle energy, which involves interactions with your environment that go beyond your physical actions, the sounds you make, and the odors you give off.

This subtle energy is easiest to conceive of as a field through which other waves of energy can flow. A good analogy would be the envelope of air that surrounds the earth. The air itself is a field of energy that is also a medium for sound waves. In a similar way your subtle energy field is a medium for emotional, mental, and other energy waves.

Some teachings call this subtle energy field the "aura," and that's as good a name as any, though I prefer the Hawaiian term, *hoaka*. In any case, it is through your aura, or *hoaka*, that you are able to exchange emotional and psychic information with other people. Intuition, premonitions, hunches, shared emotions and healing influences all operate through the medium of your subtle energy field.

The energy of your aura can be expanded, contracted, focused and channeled in a number of different ways for a number of different purposes by using the power of your mind to give it direction.

A subtle energy experience. This exercise will help to give you a tangible experience of your subtle energy.

> 1. Hold your hands about six to eight inches (15-20 centimeters) apart with your palms facing each other.
>
> 2. Inhale with your attention on your navel, and exhale with your attention centered in the space between your hands. Do this about four times.
>
> 3. Next, push your hands very slightly toward each other with a gentle bouncing motion. At this point, most people will experience a sensation of pressure, as if you were pressing against a soft balloon, and perhaps other sensations as well. If you do experience this you are feeling the effects of an intensification of your subtle energy field in the space between your hands.

When your aura is "charged" with mental and/or emotional energy it can have a strong effect on how other people perceive you. People who seem to have a lot of charisma have highly charged subtle energy fields. Although some people do this naturally without realizing what they are doing, it is also possible to do it consciously and to develop it as a skill.

Charging your aura. Here is one way to get started with

becoming more charismatic.

1. Think of your aura, or at least assume that it exists around you.

2. Use your imagination and/or memory recall to get as excited as you can. Memories of happiness, fun, or laughter work well for this.

3. Interact with people and note how they react to you when your aura is charged.

Your Source Of Energy

The subject of this section is not God, however you interpret that. Personally, I believe that there is one source for everything in the universe, but this isn't what I'm discussing now. In this section I want to talk about an aspect of yourself that extends beyond your body, your mind, or your various forms of energy. It's based on an idea that you are more than any of those, that there is a part of you that exists beyond time and space, and yet within it at the same time. You can think of it as a theory, of course, because everything we believe about anything is theoretical to someone. My concern here is not to get you to believe in what I'm talking about. It's to get you to consider using it for practical purposes. But in order to do that more effectively we have to give it a name. "Spirit" will not work because that word has too many meanings in English and does not translate well into other languages. 'Aumakua and Kane are Hawaiian words that could be used for this concept, but they also have other meanings that might confuse people. I have used Max Long's term, "Higher Self," in my writings, but I'm not really happy with it because it implies a hierarchical relationship that really isn't part of my tradition. So, I'm going to break new ground and call it your "Greater Self."

Regardless of any other consideration, the primary, practical, personal usefulness of the Greater Self is as a source of inspiration. There are other uses applicable to your relationships with other people and with the world in general, but we'll get to those later.

"Inspiration" has two important meanings in this context. One is the idea of being inspired with energy, and the other is the idea of being inspired with ideas. Thus, we can speak of a person being inspired to do something without consciously thinking about it, and we can speak of a person being inspired to think of a new way to solve a problem.

Everyone is inspired in some way at some time, and for most people it probably just happens when it happens. Some people recognize that it comes when they need it. Smart people find a way to induce it when they want it. What follows is one simple way to do that.

How to ask for inspiration. Be forewarned: this is one of those absurdly simple techniques that work anyway.

> 1. Find a quiet space and either look at or imagine something beautiful and feel how that feels.
>
> 2. Assume you have a Greater Self and ask it for inspiration, either as energy or guidance or both for something you need or want. To help your focus, you can think of your Greater Self as an invisible presence filling you, surrounding you, and extending out beyond you as far as you can imagine.
>
> 3. Trust that you will get what you ask for in some way or another.

There is no way to tell ahead of time how or when the inspiration will manifest. It may come immediately as a flash of feeling or insight, as words or images now or later, or through someone or something in your environment at a time when you are doing something else. All you have to do is to trust that it will come, and to pay attention.

I have a friend who used to own a bookstore and she told me of a time when she needed inspiration for something important in her life. As she walked down an aisle of her bookstore a book fell on her head. She was so involved with her thinking that she just reached down, picked it off the floor, and put it back on a shelf. A few days later it happened again. This time she looked at it, wondered why it didn't look familiar, and put it back on the shelf. Then it happened a third time and she finally checked her records and found she had never ordered it. The book was one of mine, *Kahuna Healing*, and it's what brought us together. Every time I ask a workshop audience if they ever needed inspiration and a book practically jumped out at them when the visited a bookstore, I almost always get a 100% response. More recently I've asked about radio and television and movies and I get a lot of positive responses from those, too. Needed inspiration can also come from children, strangers, or even billboards. I prefer to think that it comes from the Greater Self, but you can give credit to any source you choose. The most important thing is that it happens.

PART THREE

Why Can't We All Just Get Along?

CHAPTER SEVEN
HEALING FAMILY RELATIONSHIPS

Although I began with the importance of healing your relationship with yourself, the way you behave with yourself is usually learned within the context of a family group. And that usually means that most of what you know about relationships was learned from your parents.

When a mother bird lays eggs she sits on them until they hatch, and then she feeds the young until they are ready to fly. In some species the male feeds the female until the eggs hatch, and in others the male shares hatching duties and then the feeding duties. After taking good care of them up to a certain age Momma and Poppa Bird demonstrate the art of flying and encourage the young to take off. If they don't want to take off they are kicked out of the nest.

In most mammal groups the young are protected and fed and trained until they are old enough and smart enough to feed themselves, and then they are pushed away from the mother's teat and either sent off to fend for themselves or given a place in the hierarchy of the group which allows them to have group protection in return for a contribution of skills and service to the group.

Of all the animals on earth, human beings take the longest to mature. They need to be cared for and protected and trained for many years before they are ready to fend for themselves or to help support the group. In most traditional societies this process can take as long as fourteen years. What's really odd is that in modern society this process either takes many more years than that or it never seems to end. Not only do many people not want to stop being children, many people don't want to stop being parents, either.

It's understandable why many people would not want to stop being children. They are no different than the young birds who are reluctant to leave a nice, cozy nest where all their needs are taken care of. It's tough for a bird, or a mammal, or a human to get out there and take care of itself and find a mate and raise a family. Or even just take care of itself. But humans and other animals are not fully grown until they can do that. Of course, human society provides for a lot of cooperation and a lot of help. For all their faults, human beings are the most helpful creatures on earth. The more willing a person is to help himself or herself the more help he or she will find.

At first glance it is harder to understand why someone would want to maintain control over one's children long past the time when they ought to be taking care of themselves and helping to support their society. The answer is simple, though. It's fear. That's the only reason people try to control other people. There may be many reasons for the fear, but that doesn't make the control a good thing. Such parental control only serves to stunt the growth of the children, whether the "parent" is a person or a group or a government. If you love someone, don't just set them free. Help them learn how to fly first.

The Parental Dilemma

It isn't easy to be a parent. Depending on your parents, of course, it isn't easy to be a child, either. However, the reason it isn't easy to be a child is that it isn't easy to be a parent.

A very, very long time ago, when the majority of human beings were organized into tribes, clans, and/or tightly-knit family groups, parenting was a social skill that you learned along with others close to your own age and with a lot of support from relatives. Grandparents, younger siblings, uncles, aunts, and cousins all participated in the raising of children according to the standards of their particular culture. Within the extended family structure there was a general sense of personal security from knowing one's place in the group and the rules of behavior toward others in the group. Some moderately extended families today still enjoy this benefit, and the results can be seen in the overall positive behavior of the children.

Unfortunately, most of our modern, urban world isn't like that anymore. There has been so much social change and disruption all over the world that a typical family group today consists of parents and children and that's it. When there are other relatives they are typically scattered all over the place.

A major effect of this is that huge numbers of young adults get married and have children without any idea of how to raise them. I am reminded of an orphaned kitten that my family took care of when we lived on a farm. It grew into a healthy young cat and on one of its outings it encountered a male cat that had its way with her. We noticed that she was pregnant and didn't think much about it. When she was obviously close to term we prepared a comfortable box for her to have her kittens in. She gave birth to three tiny kittens without much fuss, but then she just got up and walked away. To our great puzzlement she wouldn't have anything to do with them and treated them like strangers. We finally realized that she had had no social context, no cat family experience, to help her understand what this phenomenon was all about.

Human parents who lack any child-raising experience may act in a similar way, but at least they usually have access to books and support groups if they care enough. However, my main point here is that there is a general lack of child-raising training. When people don't know what to do when they have to do something, they do the best they can. And that means they have to draw from whatever knowledge or experience they have or can find in books and support groups in order to manage the behavior of these crying, screaming, messy, demanding, rebellious, reckless, and wild things called children.

How To Handle Children

As the father of three boys and the grandfather of five girls and three more boys, all I can do is to share some of the things I've learned as they grew up.

The most important thing I can tell you is that children need love more than anything else. You can be a pitiful parent in every other way, but if you can give them enough love they will turn out fine. Not perfect, by any means, but fine.

Just thinking that you love them is not enough. Children aren't mind readers. They need to feel loved. And when they feel loved they feel more secure, and they have less need to seek love and power in strange ways and in strange places with strange people.

So, how can you make them feel loved? The truth is, you can't. In spite of your best efforts, children are going to feel however they decide to feel. Nevertheless, there are some things you can do that will greatly increase the chances that they will feel more loved than not.

Guidelines. Children need guidelines for how to behave

in the world and how to cope with the world. They do not need a whole list of rules, restrictions, and regulations designed to make the parents feel better. They need guidelines about right and wrong, about what is appropriate and inappropriate, about what works and what doesn't work, about what is legal and illegal, as best as you can give it to them. As they grow up they'll hear lots of other ideas about these things from other people, and they'll often be inclined to do a lot of testing and experimenting, but the more practical the guidelines are that you give them, the more likely they are to return to them and pass them on.

So, I would recommend explaining the reasons behind giving your guidelines from the time you first start giving them. A baby in a crib is not a blank slate. It's a human being trying to learn everything it can, as fast as possible, about how to live life effectively. Even a baby listens to what you have to say, and will respond in some degree to your explanations of why things are the way they are and why you want it to behave the way you do.

Respect. A lot of parents treat their children like slaves or servants, or even necessary inconveniences. It's probably because they themselves were treated that way. It is not a method that helps to produce happy children or effective future parents, however. Also, it does not produce respect for the parents.

True respect has to come from the heart. The external appearance of respect that comes from obedience to rules is just play-acting based on fear. True respect is given freely when it is received.

Let me clarify that by putting it another way. If you treat people, including children, with respect, they will tend to respect you. It's as simple as that.

Treating a child with respect means that when you tell a child what to do, you listen to what he or she thinks about it, and then you either change what you want or explain why you can't. This doesn't guarantee happiness or compliance, but it does establish a better relationship. Having respect for the child also means paying attention to what the child wants or does, and giving importance to his or her concerns. And it means involving the child in major family decisions. It does not mean letting the child run the family, it means acknowledging the child as a participating member of the family.

Social Contact. Human beings bond by doing things together in a way that produces emotional rapport. Just doing things together isn't enough. People who work together on a business or scientific project do not necessarily experience any degree of bonding. People who do something enjoyable or dangerous together do tend to bond.

In some families bonding is done by a lot of touching. The Italian side of my family did a great deal of hugging, and hand-shaking, and touching and kissing, in public and in private. That is not to say that they always got along with each other, but underlying any disagreements was always a strong sense of family connection. Added to that, of course, were a lot of extended family gatherings. It took my father, with his English background, and my wife, with her German/English background, quite a while to get used to all this physical contact.

In other families emotional bonding is done by participating in group activities, like sports, or hiking and camping, or parties. In others, bonding can even come about by sharing more intellectual activities.

The key factor in bonding is the emotional connection. To be effective as a means of bonding, an activity has to stimulate feelings associated with love, either enjoyment or mutual support. Bonding does not come from the activity itself, then, but from the emotional experience of the activity. An activity that stimulates bonding during one phase of family

149

interaction will not necessarily have the same effect during another phase.

For instance, just because parents and children had a good time doing something like camping together when the children were pre-teens, doesn't mean that the children will feel the same way about that activity when they are older and seeking bonds with their peers. Forcing a child to engage in an activity that he or she no longer enjoys may weaken the bond through resentment, rather than strengthen it. If the parents are flexible enough to change family activities, or even to encourage the children to enjoy positive bonding with other groups, the original family bonds will remain intact because the memories will still be enjoyable.

An exercise for parents. When children grow up and become adults they are no longer children. Unfortunately, in the eyes of many parents, their children are always children and this can get in the way of good relating. The fact that in English and other languages there is no separate word for grown-up children makes it even more difficult. The English word, "adolescent," refers to someone who is between puberty and adulthood, neither a child nor an adult. In Hawaiian, at least, there is a word, *kama*, that is used by parents to designate a child who has become an adult. Interestingly, the phrase for "adult" in Hawaiian is *kanaka makua*, meaning "parent person." However, the little exercise that follows is designed to help parents to stop thinking of their adult children as the little children they once were.

> 1. Imagine that you are in some pleasant location, indoors or outdoors, at home or elsewhere, and imagine that your children are with you as they were before they were adolescents.
>
> 2. In this pleasant place in your mind imagine your children growing into the adults that they are now.
>
> 3. Still in your mind, give each of your children a gift

to celebrate the fact that they are now adults. This could be a piece of special jewelry, a flower lei, or anything else you choose to represent this special occasion.

4. Finally, give each adult child a wish for happiness and success and send them into the world, away from your location, and out of sight. Remember, this is a symbolic departure from the state of childhood, and it does not mean that your real adult children have to go out of your life.

How To Handle Parents

Whether we like it or not, parents play a major role in shaping our lives. First and foremost, they provide the ancestral DNA that forms our bodies and deeply influences our physical, emotional, and mental growth. This is a fundamental factor in our life experience that permeates everything we do. Fortunately, it does not control us, because we are not machines, not just duplicates of our parents. We have spirit and will and the power of choice. We are the builders of our own lives, but we have to use the material given us by our parents to build with.

After birth and, in this modern technological age, sometimes before birth, we may or may not have any more direct connection with our parents. Some people are raised by their parents, some are raised by relatives, and some are adopted, officially or unofficially. In any case, the people who raise us play a parental role that influences us strongly throughout our lives. Whether we accept their ways or rebel against them, their influence remains strong. Authority figures, like teachers, leaders, idols, employers and all those who guide our behavior with or without our consent have a parental-type influence as well. I still remember my first year at the University of Colorado when I was married with a child and three years of military service behind me, and the university administrative office insisted that I get my mother's signature on a student loan form. I thought the requirement was silly because at the time I was an adult with a family helping to support my mother who had no income to speak of. However, the University had a policy for dealing with students called *in loco parentis*, which meant that in the absence of a parent the University itself would act as a parent. And that meant that if Daddy University said I needed Mommy's signature then I had to get it, regardless of the circumstances.

Parental influence has a much deeper effect than most of us realize. At one time I thought that I had rid myself of any strong parental influence on my life. I still admired and used a lot of my father's teachings, and I still ate a lot of the foods my mother had fed me, but I didn't think the influence went much beyond that. And then I learned a simple technique for looking at our relationship differently.

A parental awareness technique. You can use this for your birth parents or for any important parental figure in your life.

> 1. Think of your most important likes and dislikes, of your most important accomplishments, of your most important goals, of your most important values of right and wrong, good and bad.
> 2. Think of the same things for each of your parents, as far as your knowledge of them allows.
> 3. Find as many instances as you can of matches and opposites.

This was a huge surprise for me, because I had never considered my parents in this way before. Here are a few things that I found in relation to my father: My father loved travel and adventure, and so do I. My father had a profound interest in nature and healing and in esoteric knowledge, and so do I. My father did not like taking orders from anyone, and neither do I. My father formed an organization of people devoted to making the world a better place, and so did I. My father never did understand money, and I've gone out of my way to do so.

By the time I noticed that I had visited every country my father had ever mentioned being in I was starting to feel like a clone. But then I took some time to think of all the things that I've done that he never did, and all the places I've been to where he never went, and all the goals I have that are just different from what his were, and I realized that although his influence was strong, his ways did not govern mine. Nevertheless, the exercise can provide useful insights about your parental relationships.

The Transmogrification Syndrome. "To transmogrify" is an odd English word meaning "to change appearance or form," and a "syndrome" is a set of behaviors often used in relation to illness. As I apply it, "The Transmogrification Syndrome" refers to a curious phenomenon that often occurs when adult children visit their parents. When that happens an amazing transformation takes place. Previously competent adults transmogrify into incompetent little children. And this syndrome may appear in spite of the most determined effort on the part of the adult children not to let it happen.

Actually, the experience is due to another effect called "entrainment." When your subconscious encounters a situation in which it doesn't know what else to do, it follows habit. And when other factors in the situation, like parents, have a strong expectation that the habit behavior will be followed, the urge to do so is almost irresistible. In other words, if your parents expect you to behave as you did when you were completely under their domination, you probably will if you don't know what else to do.

Some adult children, upon discovering that the syndrome is taking effect, will try to use logic to avert it (the "If you haven't noticed I'm an adult now" technique), but that doesn't work very well, because typical parents don't even hear you when you talk like that. Other adult children will get very upset and throw tantrums, but that only compounds the problem by proving that the parents are right. There is something very effective that adult children can do about this, but it has to be done before they go home.

How to heal TS. The key phrase above was, "if you don't know what else to do." TS occurs when adult children have not learned a new set of behaviors to apply when they encounter parents who expect them to act like the little children they once were. A long-term solution is to develop such a solid sense of self confidence that you don't get entrained into the old behavior. A faster solution is to rehearse.

> 1. Think of yourself as the competent adult that you are (or imagine yourself as the competent adult you would like to be, if the former thought doesn't work for you).
>
> 2. Take some time to think of or imagine how you feel as a competent adult, how you move, and sit, and stand, and hold your body. Do this until you get a good association with the thinking and the feelings.
>
> 3. Now imagine yourself going home to visit your parents, and imagine interacting with them as the competent adult that you are. Imagine how you will respond to them, how you will speak, what you will say, and how you will act. Maintain a sense of the competent adult body movement and posture the whole time.
>
> 4. Visit your parents after having gone through this rehearsal several times. Do your best not to resist your parents' attempts to behave toward you in the old way, but instead just maintain your competent adult way of thinking, feeling, and moving.

5. Your parents may experience some confusion at first when your old pattern doesn't emerge, but they will adapt to your new persona if you are persistent. If the results of the first visit are not satisfactory, do some more rehearsal.

Abusive Parents

It's an unpleasant subject, but a chapter on family relationships wouldn't be complete without it. Abuse of children may be done by family members other than parents, of course, but we'll discuss it in terms of parents and you can modify it for other relationships. Childhood abuse can take several forms, and they'll be discussed in turn.

Verbal abuse. I think this topic and solutions for it have been covered fairly well in the chapter on Criticism and Praise.

Physical abuse. In my opinion, modern attitudes about physical abuse of children by parents have gone overboard. There is a vast difference between giving a child a sound spanking for breaking important rules, and beating a child to the point of injury out of anger or arrogance. My father told me of pretty hard whippings he received from his father, and my father didn't seem to have any serious emotional consequences from that. I was spanked by both my father and my mother when I deserved it (and my mother was sometimes pretty angry when she did it) and I turned out okay. My own children got their share of spankings when I couldn't think of any other way to change their behavior, and all of them have turned out wonderfully (they don't spank their children, though). The difference, I think, is whether the spanking is accompanied by emotional rejection or not. I didn't spank my children very often, and it was always as a last resort for behavior change, but when I did I always let them know what rules had been broken beforehand, and I always assured

155

them of my love afterward. If I had known what I know now about human behavior, spanking would never have been necessary, but my point is that in the context of a loving family it did no harm.

That said, let's turn to the problem of real physical abuse, the kind that causes serious injury and emotional trauma. Since this is a book on relationships, the primary concern here is with the residual effects of the memories of such abuse and how it affects current relationships.

The two main reactions that people have to severe childhood abuse are fear and anger. The two main effects that people have from memories of this are fear of or anger toward people of the same sex as the abuser. This happens because one of the talents of our subconscious is that of generalizing specific experiences.

As part of our survival programming, we have the ability to learn a pattern of behavior in relation to one experience, and to apply that learning to other, similar experiences. By getting our fingers burnt in one fire, we learn how not to touch other fires. By getting hurt by a father or mother, we learn to avoid men or women who remind us of them. Except that it's not that simple.

Being human, we may get curious about fire in general and learn how to use it or even walk on it. And the experience of getting hurt by a parent may lead us into finding ways of healing such people. Also, if the hurtful parent is the only source of love we have, we may subconsciously seek out such people, rather than avoid them. Human beings are very interesting.

Curiously, the lower the self esteem of a person, the more likely he or she is to be subconsciously attracted to people with the same characteristics as the parent, and the higher the self esteem of a person, the more he or she is to be subconsciously and consciously attracted to someone with characteristics that are the opposite of the abuser. If you find yourself attracted to people who turn out to be abusers, you might try raising your self esteem with some of the ideas and techniques already given.

If your problem is that you are afraid of entering into a new relationship because the person might turn out to be just like your father or mother, here is something you can try:

> 1. Bring up a memory of an abusive parent, but project it on a movie screen or see it as a photograph so you don't get emotionally involved with it.
>
> 2. Tell yourself very strongly, "This was my abusive parent (name the name if you can), a unique individual, different from any other human being on earth."
>
> 3. Continue with, "No one else I have ever known, that I know now, or that I will ever know in the future, is the same person as that person."
>
> 4. Continue with, "That was then and this is now. I will look at new relationships as what they really are, new relationships."
>
> 5. Repeat until this way of thinking feels natural or comfortable.

Emotional Abuse. Some parents are monsters, people without compassion who either delight in torturing their own children by making them fearful, or who try to put their children into a mold that they aren't suited for, against their will and for the emotional satisfaction of the parent only.

When I was in junior high school there was a very unhappy boy who looked like a miniature body-builder. He was strong and athletic and a pretty nice guy, but his father wouldn't let him socialize beyond the minimum necessary in school. His daily routine would put many athletes to shame and he had no time to just be a boy. I don't know what happened to him, except that he never became the star his father wanted him to be.

On the side of pure terror, I know of parents who forced their children to participate in very scary rituals that left them in a state of near constant panic as adults.

The effect of this kind of treatment is to have the parents almost constantly in mind along with feelings of fear or anger. Naturally, this interferes with having normal adult relationships. For this problem I am going to give you one form of The Dynamind Technique from my book, *Healing For The Millions*.

> 1. Hold your hands in front of you with fingertips touching each other.
>
> 2. Think of your parent and locate the place in your body where you feel the fear or the anger.
>
> 3. Make the following statement to yourself: "When I think of my (parent) I feel fear/anger in my (name the place in the body), and that can change. I want that feeling to go away.
>
> 4. Tap the center of your chest seven times, the top of the web of each hand between your thumb and fore-finger for the same count, and the base of the back of your neck for the same count.
>
> 5. Inhale with your attention above the crown of your head, and exhale with your attention below your feet.
>
> 6. Think of your parent again and notice if there is any change in your feelings of fear or anger. If there still is some, repeat the process.

On this same subject, there are times when a person may feel emotionally abused, but without just cause. One man I worked with felt betrayed by his mother because she left home when he was a child, and this feeling interfered with his life as an adult because he was afraid of being betrayed by another woman. For this problem we used a technique that I call a "Skinny Description."

158

1. Think of the situation that you have strong negative feelings about.

2. Change your description of the situation by stating the bare facts, without any adjectives or adverbs.

3. Notice how this changes your feelings.

In the man's case above, the first description was, "My mother betrayed me." The Skinny Description of this event was, "My mother left home and I don't know why." This changed his feelings so dramatically that he felt free of the memory for the first time.

Sexual Abuse. It's rather scary to think of how much sexual abuse there is in families. At least it seems like a lot when you are engaged in helping people with their emotional problems. There may even be more than most people realize, because in addition to those who seek help, there are those who would never dream of talking about it, and those who recover from it on their own.

For changing one's feelings about the experience and becoming free of its influence, some of the techniques already discussed will be very helpful, including those related to forgiveness and self esteem. Additionally, the following technique may also help.

The next technique is based on a private session in which a client asked me to play the role of her father for a few minutes. There was no dialogue at all, because most of the action was going on in her mind. We were in chairs facing each other when, to my surprise, she asked me to put my hand on her leg. When I did, she lifted it off and pushed it away. We repeated the process three times, then she sighed and smiled and told me it was no longer a problem. During the process, in her mind she was encountering her father at a time when her father made sexual advances. As a child she did not resist him, but as an adult she was able to rewrite the memory by imagining that, as a child, she was able to push his hand away

159

and refuse his advances. The repetition and the physical presence of my hand, helped to make the new memory stronger than the old, and her feelings about herself and about the incident were changed for the better.

1. Recall an incident of sexual abuse.

2. Imagine that you had the will and the power to refuse the advance or change the situation, and do it, vividly, in your mind.

3. Use some kind of physical movement and/or a physical prop to help reinforce your imagination.

4. Repeat the process as often as it takes to produce a change in your feelings, and every time the old memory pops up, replace it with the new memory.

How To Handle Siblings, Aunts, Uncles, And Cousins

This may be the shortest section on the book. The best way to handle these relationships is to use the same ideas and techniques that were discussed in this and previous chapters, and that are discussed in the next chapter.

CHAPTER EIGHT
FRIENDS AND FRIENDSHIP

You will only have two, or at most a few, parents in your life, plus a few more significant author- ity figures, and your other relatives may or may not be more numerous. In most cases, though, the greatest number of significant relationships in your life will be with friends. Let's start off by defining our terms.

What Is A Friend?

Some time ago I was discussing friendship with some- one and that person told me that she was very selective about whom she allowed into her circle of friendship, and so she had very few friends. Although she seemed proud of the fact, I said to her, "That's too bad. I have thousands of friends all over the world because I'm not selective at all."

We each have the right to determine for ourselves who our friends will be, and what constitutes a friend in the first place. Since I am committed to increasing love on the planet, I am admittedly biased toward increasing friendship, rather than restricting it. So, what follows are some of my basic ideas about friendship, drawing upon quotes from the Bible and Hawaiian words for related ideas.

In the Book of John, Jesus makes a profound statement about friendship. "Greater love hath no man than this, that a man lay down his life for his friends."

This statement of Jesus has become so familiar that it's easy to miss what's really being said. In context it is saying that there is no greater kind of love than friendship. Not brotherly, or sisterly, or parental or devotional or altruistic love. Friendship tops them all. The rest of the chapter contains equally important and related statements that are seldom quoted. Here's the whole thing:

> This is my commandment, that ye love one another as I have loved you. Greater love has no man than this, that a man lay down his life for his friends. Ye are my friends ... Henceforth I call you not servants, for the servant knoweth not what his lord doeth; but I have called you friends, for all things that I have heard of my father I have made known unto you.

This is a relationship of equals, the highest form of love that Jesus can offer his disciples. It is also worth noting that at other times when Jesus greets someone, even Judas, it is as "Friend." Never as "Brother" or "Sister," for instance. As a matter of fact, Proverbs 17:17 says, "A friend loveth at all times, and a brother is born for adversity." Of course, if a brother is also a friend, that changes everything.

Here are some other things worth noting from the Bible: Exodus 33:11 says "And the Lord spake unto Moses face to face, as a man speaketh unto his friend." And in the Book of James it says that Abraham was called the "Friend of God." Obviously this term was used on purpose to convey a very high kind of mutual love.

In modern times a psychological study of happiness showed that it was attained mostly by people with at least

162

one close relationship and a circle of supporting friends. An apparent anomaly in the study was that soap opera devotees tended to rank higher in happiness than non-devotees, and it has been suggested that the devotees think of the actors as their friends. The friends don't have to be people, either. Other studies show that people with pets as friends tend to be not only happier, but healthier, too.

Is there a difference between friendship and love? Apparently not. In Middle English the word "friend" means "lover," and it stems from a word in Old Gothic meaning "to love." If anything, it implies a deeper kind of love, one that goes beyond obligation.

In English, the degree of closeness of a friendship can only be suggested by adjectives, such as "a fair weather friend," "a close friend," "an intimate friend." Hawaiians had many separate words for "friend" that signified varying degrees and types of friendship. *Hoaloha* (beloved companion), for example, is a general term for friend. *Makamaka* (face to face) is a friend with whom you share freely. *Aikane* (uncertain derivation) is a close, personal friend of the same sex. *Pilialoha* (sticky love) is a romantic friend. And here's a great one: *'au ko'i* (axe handle), a trusted friend.

Ralph Waldo Emerson said, "The only way to have a friend is to be one." But many people have trouble making friends because they don't know how to be one. So here is a set of guidelines to help you remember, based on the letters of the English word, friend. The letters may not apply in other languages, but the concepts do:

F stands for Freedom. Friends do not try to control each other. I have encountered many people, clients and students, who have personal relationships that they call friendships, but which sound more like parent/child relationships when they are described. The need or desire for control comes from a need or desire for power over the other person. And this, of

163

course, comes from a fear of being powerless.

There are many ways in which one person in a close relationship may try to control the behavior of the other, but the most common way is through direct or indirect criticism. Although I already have presented a chapter on this subject, I want to cover some more ideas in this one.

Direct criticism is simply that: verbal statements that criticize another person's behavior. Often disguised euphemistically as "constructive criticism" (meaning "I'm pretending to do this for your own good, but I'm really doing it so you will do what I want you to do"), direct criticism which is frequent has a very destructive effect on the relationship, and on the self esteem of the person on the receiving end. Below are some techniques that you can use to neutralize the effect of such criticism and discourage its use. None of them are confrontational, but they will probably require practice to be effective.

Anti-Criticism Technique #1: This is one of those deceptively simple ones.

> 1. Whenever you receive a direct criticism, mentally give yourself a compliment. The compliment you give to yourself does not have to be related to the criticism.
>
> 2. It is very helpful to already have a short list of true compliments, perhaps four or five, that you can memorize for such occasions.
>
> 3. This technique helps you relieve the tension caused by the other person's criticism.

Anti-Criticism Technique #2: This technique is adapted from one called "Fogging" in the book, *When I Say No I Feel Guilty*, by Manuel P. Smith. Fogging is especially effective when someone is trying to use criticism on you in a manipulative way, trying to make you feel guilty, or trying to get you to do something you don't want to do. I have used it many times with good results.

1. When someone criticizes you, listen to the criticism and accept any part of it you choose, but under your own terms. Let's suppose that someone says, "You never do anything right!" Then you would reply with something like, "You're right. I do make too many mistakes." You see? You've accepted the criticism, but not the way it was stated. As long as you can accept the fact that you probably do make too many mistakes, that reply would work.

2. If someone says, "You just did a lousy job," you might reply, "You're right, I could have done better," if you can accept the idea that you could have done better. What you do is to modify the criticism in a way that is tolerable to you, and you acknowledge your modification, not the original criticism.

3. It's called Fogging because almost always the person criticizing is left in a fog. They know you just did something, but they can't quite figure out what it was. You are not doing this to make them feel that way, you're just doing this to make yourself feel stronger and be able to handle criticism better. It's a wonderfully powerful technique, because in the process of accepting the part that you modify, you become your own judge without having to defend yourself or become stressed at the criticism. And you do not acknowledge that anyone else has the right to judge you on their terms.

Anti-criticism Technique #3. This one will be more difficult for some people, because it requires you to accept what the other person says without modification. It is particularly suitable to situations where the criticism is specific and accurate. As a technique it greatly resembles what Smith calls "Negative Assertion" in his book, but I learned it as the

"Bamboo Technique" from my father.

> 1. When someone criticizes you specifically and accurately, acknowledge it completely. If someone says, "You promised to take me someplace and you didn't do it. You broke your promise!" Instead of defending yourself, you would say, "Yes, I did break my promise. You have a right to feel unhappy about that." You are acknowledging the criticism and you are sympathizing with the critic. Accepting full responsibility when it is justified leaves you feeling stronger and the critic less unhappy.
>
> 2. You could also say, "I'm sorry," and you could offer an explanation, but don't offer excuses.

I've had occasion to use this a number of times in my life. On one important occasion it had surprising after effects. It happened in the country of Dahomey (now called Benin) when I was Director of Socio-economic Development programs for an American voluntary agency. My counterpart in the government was the Director of Social Services, whom I'll call Mr. P. Our relationship up to this point had been one of wary acquaintances. One morning he called me to say that the Minister of Health required our presence immediately. No explanation was given, so I hurried over to the Minister's office only to find that Mr. P. had arranged the meeting for the purpose of criticizing my actions and getting me into trouble with the Minister. As I listened to Mr. P.'s litany of accusations, I remembered my father telling me that an oak tree stands firm and resists the wind, but if the wind is strong enough it blows the tree over; whereas a bamboo tree bends with the wind no matter how strong it is, and when the wind stops the bamboo hasn't changed position at all. When Mr. P.'s wind stopped, I looked the Minister in the eye and said, "Mr. P. is absolutely correct. I did every one of those things. May I tell you my purpose in doing them?" When the Minister nodded I gave a point-by-point explanation, not an excuse, for each action. Before I was finished Mr. P. threw up his hands in a dramatic gesture and said, "You see! You see, Mr. Minister. The man is like smoke! You can't grab hold of him!" The Minister laughed and dismissed up both. In the corridor, Mr. P. did something totally unexpected. He invited me out for a drink, and that was the beginning of a wary friendship.

Indirect criticism is more subtly manipulative and difficult to deal with, because disapproval is conveyed not through words, but by gesture, facial expression, and a myriad of behavior patterns that make it clear the critic is unhappy with you. The subtlety makes it hard to counteract, because our natural impulses to be liked and to cooperate with others are so strong. Even worse, a person with low self esteem may have a tendency to interpret another person's behaviors as critical even when they are not. What works best for this is purposeful, ongoing practices that increase self esteem. When self esteem is high enough, indirect criticism ceases to have any effect.

R stands for Respect. I mentioned the need for respect in regard to children in the previous chapter and the same thing applies to friends, plus more. My particular concern in this section is respect for differences. Friends don't have to be clones. Of course, in order for there to be a friendship at all there must be shared beliefs, values, and interests, but there can also be different beliefs, different values, and different interests. I have some great friends who don't believe in Huna, aren't interested in shamanism, don't care for Hawaii, and would rather have a beer than make the world a better place. But they like me and I like them and we have a good time together, because of what we do share.

Sometimes, in the course of a friendship, people take very different life paths. This often results in much less personal contact, but it doesn't have to mean an end to the friendship. There are friends that I haven't seen nor heard from in over twenty years, yet I know that if we came together again it would be a delightful experience. Friends don't always have to stay in your neighborhood.

Over the course of my lifetime there have been a few instances in which I have lost respect for a person I considered my friend. In every case it was because the person acted in a way that was contrary to one of my core values.

Everyone has a set of core values—ideas, concepts, behaviors, expectations—that are so fundamental they define our deepest sense of right and wrong, good and bad, important and unimportant. We have a lot of lesser values that define the same things, but the core values are much more powerful and more difficult to change. We feel the most rapport with people who share one or more of our core values without going against the rest, and the least rapport with people whose values or behavior go against one or more of our core values.

Most people I've met don't even think about such things, yet their core values are guiding their life and their friendships regardless. The more aware you are of your own core values, the more you will understand you own behavior and your relationships with the people around you.

A Core Value Exercise. This doesn't take very long.

> 1. Make a list of up to ten things that you would give your life for, or that you would change your life for.
> 2. Imagine situations in which such things might happen and note how you feel about it.
> 3. Try to reduce each thing to a single sentence or keyword.

I stands for Independence. A friend is someone you can depend on for something, according to the closeness or depth of the friendship. You might be able to depend on a casual friend for good conversation, and an intimate friend for help in the most dire situations you might ever get into. At the same time, it is not healthy for either of you to be too dependent on each other. You know that too much dependency is involved when you cannot be happy without the presence of your friend, or you cannot feel competent or whole without the presence of your friend. When this happens the relation ship has devolved from friendship into an addictive relationship based on a need for love and a need for power.

In such a relationship one or both of the people might be stuck in dependency. In either case it's a great strain on both people because the happiness that is supposed to be part of friendship is missing.

If you are the independent one, here is something you can do to gently disengage.

A Disengagement Technique. This will be using mind-to-mind communication.

> 1. Imagine some kind of space in which you feel comfortable, outdoors or indoors. Take some time to see and hear and feel details.
>
> 2. Mentally invite the person into your space and arrange things for a conversation. Let the person know that it is time to change the relationship, and that greater happiness awaits the person elsewhere. Imagine that the other person receives this with understanding.
>
> 3. After talking, open a door or a gate leading out of your space and onto a path that goes toward a bright light or a beautiful valley or happy group of people and imagine the person leaving your space and reaching the other destination.
>
> 4. Repeat this daily until the relationship begins to change.

If you are the dependent one and you want to get free of

your addiction, the following will be helpful.

An Independence Technique. This is also a mental technique.

> 1. Imagine a space in which you are with the other person. Say goodbye and walk away.
>
> 2. If this is difficult for any reason, such as because of emotional or physical reactions, walk away just as far as you can without distress.
>
> 3. Repeat this daily and keep increasing the distance by small amounts until you can comfortably walk away and out of sight without needing to go back.

E stands for Equality. There is no hierarchy in a friendship. Sometimes people who are in a hierarchy—social, governmental, military, religious, or whatever—do become friends with someone who is at a different level than they are, but the hierarchy and the friendship cannot co-exist in the same way simultaneously. When the hierarchy is active, the friendship is lessened, and when the friendship is active, the hierarchy is lessened. Some people can work with this alternation of roles, but for others it is too much of a strain. A king may make friends with a commoner during a hunt, but the friendship dissolves at the palace. A captain may make friends with a private during a battle, but they can't mix socially at the base. A high priest can be friends with an acolyte, but the friendship cannot be expressed in the church or the temple.

When human beings get together in unorganized groups or two or more is it natural for an informal hierarchy of leaders and followers to develop. With friends, however, this informal hierarchy is constantly shifting its leadership. This can be easily observed at a casual party where people exchange roles as they tell stories or lead activities. If you are in a relationship with one or more people where one person is always in charge, then although the relationship might be friendly, it is not a relationship of friends.

N stands for Nurture. To nurture a friend is to provide support and encouragement for that person's growth and development. This could take the form of physical, emotional, mental, financial, or social support, depending on the nature of the friendship and the capabilities of the friends. Encouragement that promotes a friend's growth and development, though, can be given under any circumstances.

When you are with a friend, then it's simply a matter of expressing your encouragement with the appropriate words and gestures. When you are separated from your friend for the time being, you can still help in a different way, using the concept that you are always connected through your spirit.

How to bless a distant friend. This kind of nurturing is what I call a blessing. By my definition that means an energized focus on something that your friend wants or needs. It can be done at any time, but I like to bless my friends in the morning soon after I get up. Here is one way to do it.

1. Look at something beautiful to harmonize your own energy, and then think of your friend.

2. Imagine your friend surrounded by a field of energy, perhaps a bright, colored light or some beautiful music.

3. Mentally state your blessing as specifically as is practical. The thing to remember is that you always bless a good thing that you want to strengthen or increase. So, you could say, "I bless your health, happiness, and success today," or, if there is a more specific need or desire, something like "I bless the success of your job interview."

D stands for Devotion. A devoted friend is one who is loyal and helpful whenever, wherever, and for as long as he or she is able to be. A devoted friend would not use friendship as an excuse to try and make another person do something contrary to what that person believes is good or bad, right or wrong. A lot of people in the world think they are doing bad things out of friendship, when they are really doing them our of a fear of being criticized for "not being a friend." Friends do not get their friends into trouble or put them in harm's way for selfish purposes.

Devoted friends are also forgiving friends. Forgiveness is a vitally important topic for all kinds of relationships, and you can re-read the chapter on forgiveness in terms of friendship if you like.

The Hawaiians made such an art of making friends that I'll end this chapter with one of their proverbs describing a good friendship:

Pili kau, pili ho'oilo
Together in the dry season, together in the wet season

CHAPTER NINE
LOVERS AND SPOUSES

The title of this chapter is not meant to imply that lovers can't be spouses, or that spouses can't be lovers. Of course they can. Except when they can't. Also, the word, lover, in this chapter may be interpreted in terms of any type of romantic relationship, and the word, spouse, may refer to any type of domestic partnership, although my comments and suggestions may be biased toward relationships between a man and a woman. In addition to whatever else is said below, both lovers and spouses could benefit greatly from studying the previous section on self esteem and the chapter on Friends and Friendship.

The Life Of Lovers

When we describe two people as being "lovers" in the English language, the implication is very strong that they are having sex together. If we say they are "in love," then the range of relationship possibilities expands considerably, because people "in love" aren't necessarily "lovers." Curious, isn't it? In any case, in this section on "lovers" I'm going to talk about different relationships of people "in love."

That urge. The urge to move toward a much closer, more physically intimate relationship with another person begins around puberty, when hormones are changing and bodies are being prepared for making and bearing children. For some strange reason, human beings are designed, intelligently or not, to get an extraordinary amount of pleasure from the sexual act, and all the activities leading up to it. The fact that they often don't is not the fault of the designer. Religious and cultural beliefs and practices have the most to do with that.

In addition to the pleasure of the act, the urge to connect with someone to do it is incredibly powerful and influences a great deal of human behavior. Beliefs about it, however, can distort a lot of that behavior. So can suppressed knowledge about it.

I recall a Charlie Brown cartoon in which the littlest kid, Linus, is telling his sister about a cute little girl that he found attractive on his first day of school. "Did you talk to her?" asked Lucy. "No," said Linus. "Then what did you do?" asked Lucy. "I hit her!"

It was funny because so many people can relate to it. For the most part, people are taught very little about what to do and how to behave when they feel that attractive urge for another person, and so they often do weird things, even as adults.

Part of the problem is certainly physiological, though, because sometimes the urge can be so strong that it clouds good judgment. Here's one version of the problem from my novel, Dangerous Journeys, in which two women are sharing a joke:

After God made man he said to the new creature, "I have given you the means to have dominion over the earth and to go forth and multiply, but there's a little problem." "What's the problem?" asked the man. "Well, to do that I had to en-

174

dow you with a brain and a penis," said God. "What could be wrong with that?" queried the man. God looked embarrassed. "The problem is that they don't ever work at the same time."

Men, and probably women, too, understand the problem very well. On the other hand, I recently read a news report about a newlywed female schoolteacher who started a love affair with a fourteen-year-old boy during a class outing, so it is not only a male problem.

I don't have a solution to the problem, except to say that if adolescents could be taught the emotional and mental effects of "The Urge" as well as the physical side it might be helpful. So might some training in self esteem and in thinking about the consequences of one's actions. Besides, it isn't always a problem. I also read recently about a couple who eloped to get married when the girl was fourteen and the boy was seventeen. Family and friends were all against it, and everyone predicted it couldn't last. The article was actually featuring their seventieth wedding anniversary, and both of them were still very much in love.

How to know when you're in love

This is very confusing for many people, because of the close links between sexual attraction and other attractions. Let's explore these things that attract people to each other.

Sexual Attraction. From the point of each individual, some people are more sexually attractive than others. There are those who think that sexual attraction has to do with how beautiful or handsome or good-looking someone is, but that isn't so. Everyone's attention is attracted to beauty as they define it, but that's primarily a cultural and social perception. Remember the Dassantch of Ethiopia and their "cattle cosmetics." Good looks and cosmetics and clothing and jewelry are used to attract attention, but all that does is to give sexual attraction an opportunity to occur.

People have many motivations for having sex, including political, economic, social, emotional and mental reasons, and many ways of stimulating their own sexual energy level, but sexual attraction between two people is awakened by energetic resonance between those people. Think of the following as a metaphor. Within our personal energy fields, each of us has a particular sexual frequency, vibrating quietly or strongly at any given moment and sending waves out into our environment. When we encounter someone else whose sexual frequency waves are in some degree of harmonic resonance with our own, the level of energy is amplified for both. The amplification may be mild, as when we find ourselves slightly turned on by someone at a party, or it can be wild, like the ninety-foot rogue waves that are formed sometimes at sea when two waves from different storms meet at exactly the same place at the same time.

I had an incident like that with a complete stranger. I was attending a healing circle organized by some kind of organization a long time ago, and I was seated between a man on my left and a reasonably attractive woman on my right. Both of them were strangers and I didn't speak to either of them. When it came time to start we held hands, and the moment my hand touched that of the woman on my right, I was overwhelmed by an incredible surge of sexual energy, accompanied by a vivid vision of the two of us making love. I think it only lasted a few seconds, because my attention was brought back to the room by the man on my left, who said in a startled voice, "What was that?" When I asked him what he meant, he said that he felt a wave of energy rushing across his lap. When I glanced at the woman she looked shaken, but we didn't speak to each other. Even later, during the socializing, it was evident that we were both feeling something for each other. I was, shall we say, not thinking with my brain and gave serious consideration to getting together with her. Fortunately, that night I had a vivid dream in which I was shown the negative consequences of such behavior and I never made contact with her again, not did she try to contact me.

The point is, strong sexual attraction can happen any time, anywhere, but it doesn't mean that you are supposed to do anything about it. It's just an energy effect. People who are strongly sexually attracted to each other may have great sex, but they may not have anything else in common, and may not even like each other.

Once in a while, during a workshop presentation, a woman may tell me that she feels a strong sexual attraction for me. Sometimes it really is a sexual attraction, because I feel it, too, but more often it is her interpretation of the excitement she felt from what I call my "workshop energy." In either case, I use the RTS technique to keep things calm. Naturally, you have to make your own choices about what to do when sexual attraction occurs, but if you don't want to do anything then this technique can help.

The RTS Technique. This technique came out of an experience that I had on Kauai when my friend and colleague, Susan, and I were waiting on a street corner to be picked up by my wife, Gloria. Susan went into a restaurant to get an ice cream cone, and she offered me some when she came out. At the time, Gloria and I were experimenting with a very strict diet that definitely did not include ice cream. Nevertheless, it was a hot day, so I took one lick of the ice cream. A few moments later she offered me another taste and I politely refused. "How can you not take another bite of this delicious ice cream?" she asked, astonished. "Simple," I told her, "I'm keeping my shoulders so relaxed that I can't lift my arms to hold the cone." So, RTS stands for "relax the shoulders." It works well for diets, and also when someone offers you a tempting sexual experience and you don't want to get involved. Keep your shoulders so relaxed that you can't lift your arms, and you'll be less like to get into trouble. Also, if the person claims to be having sexual fantasies about me, I say, "Great, enjoy them."

Emotional Attraction. Emotional attraction is not the same as sexual attraction, but when the two go together it makes for wonderful loving. Emotional attraction is also what keeps good friends together, and it is the reason why good lovers can also be good friends, but good friends don't have to be lovers.

The specific emotion involved is simple happiness. Energetically, it works a lot like sexual attraction, in that when you are in the right harmonic emotional resonance with someone their presence, or just the thought of them, makes you feel happy.

At this point I want to lay aside a myth that is too often promoted by poets, by novelists, by movies, and by musical lyrics, and that is the myth that love is painful. In one movie I saw, the heroine punches the hero hard enough for him to complain, and she says, "Love hurts." Then she kisses him. Many people relate to that because they've accepted the myth. Songs talk about the "heartbreak of love," and novels describe love as a state in which the mind spins, the heart throbs, the stomach is full of butterflies, and the knees are trembling, which sound more like vitamin deficiency to me. Many people actually believe that jealousy, heartache, anxiety, and sadness are signs of love, and they even measure the love in a relationship by the presence of those feelings.

Let's wake up, folks! This is all a distortion of love fostered by people who don't know how to love. The essence of love is feeling good. Even Webster's Encyclopedic Unabridged Dictionary of the English Language has only good things to say about love, and it emphasizes the affection aspect of

178

it. My preference, of course, is for the Hawaiian definition found in the word, *aloha*. As a word it contains meanings of love, affection, compassion, mercy, sympathy, kindness, charity, and greeting. In its roots of *alo* it means "presence," or "one who is esteemed," and *oha*, meaning "affection, love, greeting, to show joyous affection or friendship." Here, too, good feeling predominates as a characteristic of love, and feelings are emotions.

When two people like each other their auras act like attracting magnets. It is not easy to see the energy, but it is very easy to see and experience the effect. In some of my workshops I demonstrate this by inviting two people up on the stage who have declared that they like each other very much. It doesn't matter whether they are men or women or couples or friends. When they are on the stage I have them stand back to back about a foot (30 cm) apart, and then I have them think about how much they enjoy each others' company. Invariably, when they have the kind of relationship that makes them happy together, they will be drawn backward toward each other until their backs collide, without any conscious effort. Next time you are walking with someone you like, pay attention to how often you seemingly inadvertently brush up against or bump into each other. That is emotional attraction at work.

Mental Attraction. This is much more subtle than either sexual or emotional attraction, but the energetic structure is the same. There is a proverb to the effect that "great minds think alike," and they attract each other, too.

While sexual and emotional attraction are enough for short-term or occasional love affairs, long term loving also requires some mental rapport. Even long term friendships require some mental rapport, a certain number of shared ideas, beliefs, and values. In fact, some friendships exist by mental resonance only, but that's not enough for lovers.

Mental agreement does not have to exist in all ideas, beliefs and values that two people have, but the more basic agreement there is, the more creative and intellectually stimulating the relationship will be. My wife and I are friends first, lovers second, and spouses third. Our strong, mutual mental attraction enhances all three forms of relationship, and we provide creative stimulation for each other in many ways. However, if I try to discuss philosophy with her she falls asleep, if I try to tell her about my latest computer game she gets a blank look on her face, if I try to interest her in the fine points of Hawaiian grammar she finds something else to do. On the other hand, if she tries to involve me in shopping I find a place to sit and wait for her, if she tries to discuss the fine points of biometrics for the elderly my eyes glaze over, if she wants to look at houses I find something else to do (that doesn't always work, though). Still, we have enough areas of rapport that the areas where we don't have rapport don't matter in terms of how we relate to each other. When we want to do those things, we either do them alone or find someone else to do them with.

Spiritual Attraction. To tell the truth, I have mixed feelings about this. To tell the whole truth, I find that a lot of other people do, too. The problem, of course, arises because of all the different ideas that people have about what "spiritual" means.

Some people think of it in terms of "finding a soulmate." For those of you who don't know, one version of this theory is that in the form of spirit we are whole, but as we are conceived we split into two souls, and the purpose of life is to find your "twin soul" and automatically join together in blissful harmony. Well, hey, if that works for you, fine. It seems to me, though, that it's not a very efficient system, because the world appears to have too many souls who are not able to find each other. I also became a little skeptical of this theory when a spiritual teacher I knew announced to the world that he had found his soulmate, and they were married shortly after. A few years later they divorced and the teacher announced to the world that he had found his "new" soulmate. Go figure.

Another version of this theory says that for every person in the world there is one perfect person who is destined to be your soulmate, and if you can find him or her you will discover how blissful love can be. I know people who have spent and are spending their lives searching for this perfect person, and while they look they avoid committing to anyone else, even when the sexual, emotional, and mental attractions are good, because the one they are with isn't perfect. And all the ones I know who have followed this theory are fundamentally unhappy with their life. This is not surprising when you consider how much time they must spend making negative comparisons with the person at hand and their ideal. If they could take the attitude of the leprechaun in the play/movie Finian's Rainbow, they could be much happier: "When I'm not near the girl I love, I love the girl I'm near."

Another way of looking at spiritual attraction is in terms of telepathic attraction. In this theory, if you focus and affirm and visualize the kind of person you want, then he or she will be magnetically attracted to you by your telepathic broadcast. Here's how you do it:

> 1. Make a list of the qualities you want in a soulmate (or a lover or a spouse). Add pictures and symbols to represent those qualities.
>
> 2. Sit quietly and affirm strongly (make a statement) that this person will come, or is coming, into your life right now.
>
> 3. Imagine the two of you enjoying life together.

The good new is that it usually works, if you can eliminate enough of your fears and doubts. The bad news is twofold: a) the person will not always have all the qualities on your list, and will always have qualities not on your list. Whether this works for you depends on how flexible you are; and b) when the person comes into your life, he or she may not want to stay in your life. The factor here is whether or not you are the kind of person that person would want to be with.

It's amazing to me how many people ignore this side of the relationship equation. They set up all these rules and conditions for the kind of person they want to attract, and do nothing to be the kind of person that would attract the person they want. I suggest that people who want to do this give it some thought and also make a list of changes they could make in their own thinking, behavior and appearance in order to make it work.

Then there's the "no accident" theory that I ascribe to. I tend toward the idea that Spirit gives us opportunities to meet possible friends, lovers, and spouses who resonate with our energy patterns and potentials at given moments in our life. In that sense, they are spiritually attracted to us. Then, however, it's up to us to do something about it, and that's where the hard work of relating comes in. When I first met my wife we had an instant attraction for each other on several levels. In the course of our seven-year courtship, however, there were many occasions when each of us came close to moving away from each other and following another path, and each time we decided not to.

Now, some people would take that as proof that we were fated for each other, but I do not believe in such fate. We did not stay together under the compulsion of destiny, we stayed together because of choices we made out of our own free will.

I will not speak for my wife, but here are two experiences from my side. The first one I'll mention was a time when it felt to me that we were within a hair's-breadth of splitting up. Then I made the choice not to give up. "I will end up marrying you no matter how long it takes, no matter what you do," I told her. "I will not give up even when you are walking down the aisle with another man, and even if you get married to someone else I will not give up." Right now it sounds a little extreme, I admit, but it was a passionate moment. The second time I'll mention was just before I finished my military service. A friend of mine and I were planning a sailing voyage through the South Pacific when we got out. It was a serious venture and I was very excited about it. Then the time of choice came. Do I go on this great adventure of a lifetime, or do I go home and continue wooing the woman I love. There was no guarantee that the adventure would be successful, although there was no doubt that it would be an adventure. There was no guarantee that my wooing would be successful, either, and no doubt that it would be difficult. Nevertheless, when the time came to choose, I decided to take the greater risk, and went home to woo. Which turned out to be the best possible choice I could have made, and an even greater adventure than the one I had planned.

My main point here is that loving relationships do not just happen. Their continuance is based on daily choices of how to act and how to react, on daily decisions about what it important and what is not important. And if you think it's hard to be lovers, wait until you get married.

Spouses

Marriage is a curious cultural phenomenon. Some form of it occurs everywhere in human societies. Originally, it was probably the result of emotional bonding that occurred after, or during, the sexual attraction. Later it became the focus of a family group for the raising of children and for economic security. At some point the marriage bond became important enough to be a cause for celebration, or to be part of a more general celebration to ensure the fertility of the social group and/or the land. The link between the fertility of the humans and the fertility of the land was very important in ancient Europe, but not in Hawaii. Humans and elemental gods each took care of their own fertility in ancient Polynesia.

Springtime, when plants and animals gave birth to new life, became the primary time for nuptials in the temperate zones of the planet. In Hawaii, within the tropics and not having a specific season of spring, formal marriage was typically held on the eleventh night of the moon, which was called Huna. In the roots of this word are references to male and female energy.

In time, the political benefits of marriage as a means of bonding family and tribal groups became appreciated by the leaders of societies in many parts of the world, and even among commoners in some places. The legal aspects of marriage, involving bride price, dowries, the sharing of property, and inheritance probably began at this time also. Religious involvement in marriage for people in general came quite late in the Western world. Of course, religions got involved in the marriages of politically important people very early, but it was not until the twelfth century A.D. that the Christian church in Europe even acknowledged ordinary marriages, and centuries later before it became a sacrament.

In modern times marriage is in a very confused state. Governments have taken control of marriage because of its economic impact on society. Religious involvement only continues in terms of individual beliefs and in those areas where religions have political power. Multiple marriages are outlawed in most places, but, especially in Western nations, serial marriages (one after the other) are very common, and divorce—a process far more difficult than marriage because of economic considerations—has become a major industry. On top of all that, the very definition of marriage as a union between a man and a woman has come into question.

In spite of all this, from the beginning until now, the fundamental factor in any sort of marriage is the ability of two individuals to join together harmoniously in a commitment to form an enduring relationship.

I am not concerned in this book with the purpose of the marriage. It doesn't matter if the marriage is based on politics, economics, convenience, raising children, or profound love, it still involves two people who have to find some way to get along with each other. It doesn't even matter if it's a multiple marriage, there will still be two people in the group who have to get along. Nor does it matter whether the couple is composed of a man and a woman, two women, or two men, because the same concepts will apply.

In what follows, I am arbitrarily making several assumptions, as is my right since it's my book:

1. A couple of people in an enduring, live-in relationship want to get along better, or at least one of them does.

2. Ideas and techniques from previous chapters will apply to spousal relationships, so I won't have to repeat them.

3. The ideas and techniques presented may apply to anyone, even if I use male/female examples or talk about marriage as the relationship.

With that out of the way, I am going to use a problem-oriented format for this section.

Who is this person? Some people get married within a few days or weeks of meeting each other, so it's hardly surprising when difficulties arise as they discover things about the other person that they didn't know. Everyone of marriageable age has already developed a variety of habits, predilections, and idiosyncrasies that may not be compatible with the new mate. Didn't you know that your spouse liked to nibble on snacks in bed? That he or she couldn't sleep unless the room was very hot or very cold? That he couldn't stand broccoli? That she didn't know how to cook? That he dropped his underwear on the floor? That she would use any razor at hand to shave her legs?

There is no way to know everything about a person before a marriage, even if you've known that person for a long time, or even if you've lived together for a long time. Gloria and I had known each other for seven years before we got married, and had dated for most of that time. Yet, we were in for a lot of surprises in our first year of marriage.

Right after we got married in the State of Michigan we moved to Boulder, Colorado where I enrolled in the university while she worked in a hospital near Denver. Our first surprise together was a rather mild one that came up when we went looking for our first apartment and realized that neither of us knew what the other one liked or expected in a place to live. After some discussion, we narrowed our needs down to the basics. I insisted on a shower, and she insisted on a refrigerator with a freezer. When we found that combination we settled in, because anything else about the apartment that wasn't good was just an inconvenience.

A big surprise for Gloria was my choice of a major area of study for my last two years of undergraduate school. At the University of Michigan I had been enrolled in Russian Studies. When I went to enroll in the same course of study at the University of Colorado, I had trouble communicating what I wanted to the head of the Russian Department (who wanted me to do what he wanted). In frustration, I went to the head of the Asian Studies Department, who was in charge of a lot of different departments, to try and resolve the problem. Although that was the beginning of a long and fruitful friendship, I really can't remember what happened in his office. All I do know is that I came out signed up for Chinese Studies. When I went home and told Gloria, she seemed to accept it quietly, but years later she told me that she was profoundly shocked. Nobody changes his major in his junior year, she thought. Who is this man I married?

My big surprise took place in the bathroom. We were under a lot of stress trying to balance work, and schooling, and marriage, so maybe that's why it affected me so much. Anyway, there I was one early morning when I suddenly noticed the toothpaste tube that we shared in common. To my horror, she had squeezed the tube in the middle to get the toothpaste out, and had left it that way! No one in their right mind squeezes the toothpaste tube in the middle. Everyone knows that you're supposed to roll it up from the bottom. What kind of person did I marry? I found myself getting very upset, but fortunately my shamanic training kicked in, because one of the things I had been trained to do was to use my anger as a signal to change my anger. That process is a very simple one that resembles a post-hypnotic suggestion. All you do it to get very relaxed and repeat to yourself that every time you get angry you will do something to change the anger. Changing the anger itself is more interesting. The technique I used in the bathroom was one that my father had taught me called "Sitting On The Moon."

> 1. When an incident happens that makes you angry, imagine yourself sitting on the moon and looking at the earth.
>
> 2. Let yourself realize how unimportant the incident was from that point of view.
>
> 3. Take a deep breath, go back to the incident, and handle it differently.

The technique I used to handle it differently was the "Permission Technique," in which I grandly gave her permission to squeeze the tube any way she wanted to (of course I didn't tell her that at the time). That dissipated my anger very well. Some months later I surprised myself by discovering that I had picked up her squeezing habit.

Do it now/Do it later. For any couple to get along they have to share some critical core values, but each one of them will have a lot of non-critical values that can make getting along together irritatingly difficult at times.

We can have non-critical values about a wide range of things based on how our parents did things, what we've read in books or seen in movies, habits of likes and dislikes, and many other things. In a long term relationship these values held by each person have numerous opportunities to bump into each other, causing various degrees of upset according to current stress levels. However, we each have a lot of non-critical values that may not bump into anything.

For instance, when my stress levels are up I get very irritable and snappish if I'm hungry. There were times in my youth when I frequently had to go hungry, and stress in the present brings out a subconscious fear related to it. Fortunately, it doesn't bother Gloria because she doesn't give my reaction any importance. The fact that I'm quickly over it makes it even less important. When she is under stress she tends to misplace things, but that doesn't bother me because I have no values of any importance attached to that.

When it comes to doing tasks, though, our non-critical values bump rather hard. When she wants something done she wants it done then, regardless of what I'm doing or what my plans are. She will usually badger me about it until I give up and do what she wants (which could be anything from taking out the trash to repairing a shelf or washing the car). Sometimes, however, I will dig in and refuse to do it in that moment, but promise to do it later (and I often keep those promises). She gets very irritated when I do that and usually does the task herself, which irritates me because she didn't wait for me to do it when I was ready. The funny thing is, the reverse often happens when I want her to do something. Then, sometimes, she puts it off and I end up doing it (somehow that doesn't bother her).

The types of values mentioned above are just examples. Every couple will have their own non-critical value sets that bump into each other from time to time. It is a problem only when what people don't like about each other becomes more important than what they do like about each other. This tends to happen when the good aspects of a relationship are taken for granted or forgotten. If that process is left unchecked, it is all too easy for excessive criticism to raise its ugly head and destroy the marriage.

What can you do about that? I can only tell you what works in my marriage, and what I know has worked for many others. What Gloria and I do can simply be called "Daily Blessing."

> 1. Shortly after we get up we do a kind of informal blessing ritual in which we praise all the good qualities we like about each other, give appreciation to our home and environment, and send good wishes out to all the people we care about.
>
> 2. Throughout the day we always make it a point to say "Please" and "Thank you" in our dealings with each other.
>
> 3. We frequently say "I love you" during the day, kiss each other when parting even for a little while, and always say "I love you," kiss, and wish each other good dreams at night (unless I fall asleep first).

Believe me, it helps to keep all the little irritations from becoming big ones.

Mind-Reading. I never knew there were so many active clairvoyants in our society until I began doing a lot of couple counseling. The trouble is, none of them are very good clairvoyants.

When anyone in a relationship begins to assume that he or she knows what the other person is thinking, then problems in communicating are already in play. The best clairvoyants in the world can't do that on a daily basis in a close relationship, much less untrained dabblers. When you assume that you know what your partner is thinking, all you are really doing is overlaying memories of previous behavior onto current interaction. Oh, you might be accurate sometimes in certain circumstances if you know a person well and that person is a slave of habit, but in most cases you will be wrong because people grow and change whether you notice or not.

I was once the houseguest of a woman friend and her husband. The woman was very active in metaphysical affairs and the husband was in charge of a local government facility. Over dinner one night she happened to mention that her husband had no interest in or understanding of metaphysical things. Here husband didn't say anything. Late in the evening on a different night her husband and I were along and had a change to get to know each other better. It turned out that he had a profound wealth of metaphysical knowledge and ideas, but because of his wife's assumption he never got to talk to her about them. As a result she missed out on the possibility of deeper communication with her husband and even learning from him.

The worst cases of false mind-reading, as far as the mind-reader is concerned, are when someone imagines that the partner is angry with them or thinking angry thoughts about them or is criticizing them when it isn't the case. This has its roots in low self esteem, and may cause the mind-reader to destroy the marriage without cause.

Almost as bad is when one partner tries to force the other partner to do the mind-reading. This is nothing more than a form of manipulation, but the effects can be devastating on the person being forced into it and on the relationship. There are a lot of ways in which someone can do this, but in every case you are made to think that you are an idiot or that you have done something wrong if you do not know by telepathy what the person wants or how the person feels.

If someone tries to force you into mind-reading by expecting you to know what they are thinking because of their gestures or facial expressions alone, you have the right to say, "I don't understand what you mean." Often such a person will use the classic phrase, "If you don't know, I'm not going to tell you," which is exquisitely designed to make you feel incompetent and inadequate. You can just step back and say, "No, I'm not going to read minds," if you have enough self esteem. It's important to learn not to be afraid of other people's gestures and expressions and realize what they really are. Look at them factually. They are gestures and expressions only. But you may need some mental practice beforehand to be able to react differently to this.

Express your anger—carefully. There are times in a couple relationship when one person may get very angry at the other. It may be due to stress, broken rules, or something else, but it puts a great strain on relating. There are many different ways for couples to handle this, depending on the personalities involved.

Some people handle a partner's angry outbursts by not taking it personally. This can work very well, but it isn't common.

Some people react by yelling back, and some couples use this as a means of communication and letting off steam without any ill effects. This is also uncommon. More common is the situation where one partner yells, the other yells back, and the yelling escalates until they either get into a fight, or one or both just leave the scene. In the latter case, a healthy outcome is when they make up, but that doesn't always happen.

The most common situation is when one partner gets angry but holds it in without expressing it, or when the partner being yelled at gets angry but holds it in without expressing it. Either case can lead to a bigger and possibly more violent outburst from the one who held the anger back, or to a break-up of the relationship.

In order to learn the best way for you to handle anger in your relationship, you have to pay attention to your partner's anger-related behavior. In the field of anger management, one of the popular therapeutic approaches proposed by therapists is to have you express your anger to your spouse, air your grievances so that your partner knows why you are feeling angry. Yeah, right. I hate to disappoint you, but that only works if your partner is a saint or an angel, or if he or she has such a high self esteem that they are able to hear your anger without taking it personally. Unfortunately, not too many people are married to saints or angels or people with such high self esteem. Expressing your anger openly to most people results in them expressing anger back, or with them building up resentment toward you. Even the ancient Hawaiians were smarter than that. In the family therapy system of *ho'oponopono*, anger was only allowed to be expressed through a third, neutral, party.

The expression of anger in a relationship is always to due to some kind of power issue. It happens when one of the partners is feeling powerless about something, or when one's power seems threatened. This is why expressing your anger so often makes the other person angry in turn.

Unless you know for sure that expressing your anger to your partner will not have any bad consequences, it's better not to do it. However, it may be just as bad to hold it in. Not only will this result in a continuous build-up of stress in yourself, it will eventually diminish the bond of the relationship. Here are some ideas:

    1. Forgive (see Chapter Three).

    2. Express your anger to a photo of the person, then

forgive.

3. Express your anger to a rock or a tree (they don't care, but they will listen) and then forgive.

These techniques will work, but only if you would rather be happy than be right. If the brief feeling of power you get from expressing your anger to a person you know will respond in kind is more important to you than the bond of the relationship, then I can't help you.

Bridging the Gap. Sometimes the stresses of life reach a point where physical tension dampens emotional responses and one or both people in a relationship begin to feel like there is an every-widening gap between them. When that happens, all the attractions that keep people together seem to fade away. Men can get so involved in work, convincing themselves that they are doing it for their family, that they ignore their family and wonder why the marriage fails. Women can feel so abandoned by their spouse that they close down their feelings and seek other ways to relieve their stress. The only way out of this is for one person in the relationship to make the effort to bridge the gap, and, admittedly, this isn't always easy.

When Gloria and I first went to Africa, we left an active life of graduate school, social activities, and employment. Our post was in Cotonou, Dahomey (Benin today) and our home was in a tiny village across the river from Cotonou. It's very hard to describe what our new life was like to people who have never been there, but I'll give a few indications.

From an urban American environment we found ourselves in a short time where the language was different (French was the official language, of which I spoke a little and Gloria none), the food was different (goat was our main source of meat, although we occasionally got horse), bugs were rampant (I got malaria and we became indifferent to roaches), medical care was nearly non-existent (I couldn't even figure out how to open a French ampoule of medicine), the average temperature was 95°F (35°C) and the average humidity was 95%, and drums were beating twenty-four hours a day from some source we never discovered. On top of that, I had to learn a job I wasn't prepared for and which sometimes took me away from home for weeks at a time, and Gloria was stuck at home with our two-year-old son and the houseboy, with no friends to talk to.

After six months we were like strangers who lived under the same roof and shared the same bed, without any emotional contact and very little conversation. She had no understanding of my work, and I had no concept of her sense of isolation, but I did know that the marriage was going downhill fast. I made the decision that I wanted this to change, and I took the initiative to change it. First, we needed to communicate and we had to have something to communicate about, so I began the journey back to love by borrowing news magazines from the US Embassy, reading them to her in the evening, and practically forcing her to make comments on the stories. Then I started playing chess and card games with her, found someone to teach her French, and hired her as my secretary to get her out of the house and among people. By that time more young Americans our age with the Peace Corps and the embassy came to live there and a reasonable social life began.

I know that this was a rather extreme case, but it illustrates the fact that someone has to make changes when stress gets in the way of happiness. Even in the best of circumstances couples can lose contact with each other from the stresses of work and family life. When life gets too hectic for too long, I recommend making appointments with each other for fun time, and I mean actually scheduling it in to your personal calendars. Some people think it is ridiculous to schedule appointments with your spouse, but Gloria and I have done it on occasion because it works.

The whole problem of bridging the gap reminds me of a song called "Escape" by Rupert Holmes, which is usually called "The Piña Colada Song." In it, a man is sitting in bed with his wife asleep next to him. He is reading the newspaper and thinking about the fact that the spark had gone out of their marriage. Then, in the "Personals" column he reads a letter from a woman who is looking for a man who likes Piña Coladas and "getting caught in the rain," among other things, and invites the right man who reads the letter to escape with her to a new life. The man replies with a personal ad in the same paper which says that he, too, likes Piña Coladas and other things, and invites the woman writer to meet him at a bar to plan their escape. Well, as he's waiting, in walks his wife, the writer of the first letter. They discover they neither of them knew they liked Piña Coladas and the other things, so they plan their escape to a new life. It was a roundabout way to communicate, but it worked. At least in the song.

Divorce. Sometimes marriages just don't last. It's a terrible thing, but it's a fact of modern life. However, it isn't as common as we've been led to believe.

While it does appear that the United States has the highest divorce rate in the world, the commonly quoted statistic that 50% of all marriages in the U.S. end in divorce is not only highly misleading, it isn't true.

Even though the latest statistics, which date from 2003, indicate a divorce rate of less than 40%, that is also misleading. Here is an important quote from an article by Dan Hurley in The New York Times dated April 19, 2005:

> …researchers say that this is misleading because the people who are divorcing in any given year are not the same as those who are marrying, and that the statistic is virtually useless in understanding divorce rates. In fact, they say, studies find that the divorce

rate in the United States has never reached one in every two marriages, and new research suggests that, with rates now declining, it probably never will.

That's the good news. Unfortunately, divorces still happen too frequently, and the process is not only time-consuming and expensive, it often ends in bitterness between the former partners.

I don't have any quick-fix techniques to prevent a divorce, but perhaps knowing the common causes of divorce, and the common factors in a happy marriage will help.

First, the most common reasons given as grounds for divorce. These come from an article published by the American Academy of Matrimonial Lawyers and are based on information from France and the United States dated between 1969 and 1998:

Poor communication.

Financial problems.

A lack of commitment to the marriage.

A dramatic change in priorities.

Infidelity.

Failed expectations or unmet needs.

Addictions and substance abuse.

Physical, sexual, or emotional abuse.

Lack of conflict resolution skills.

Time, sex, money (the biggest obstacles for young couples).

Another study by Jeffry H. Larson, chairman of the Brigham Young University Family and Marriage Therapy Program divides the factors that contribute to an unhappy marriage, and which may lead to divorce, into the following three categories.

The first has to do with individual traits:

1. High neurotic traits.

2. Anxiety.

3. Depression.

4. Impulsiveness.

5. Self-consciousness.

6. Vulnerability to stress.

7. Anger/hostility.

8. Dysfunctional beliefs.

The second involves what the professor calls "Couple traits:"

1. Dissimilarity.

2. Short acquaintanceship.

3. Premarital sex (especially a lot of experience with many different partners).

4. Premarital pregnancy.

5. Cohabitation.

6. Poor communication and conflict-resolution skills.

The third involves the context of the marriage:

1. Younger age.

2. Unhealthy family-of-origin experiences.

3. Parental divorce or chronic marital conflict.

4. Parental or friends' disapproval.

5. Pressure to marry.

6. Little education or career preparation.

In contrast, Professor Larson lists the factors that will most likely produce a happy marriage:

Individual traits:

1. High self-esteem.

2. Flexibility.

3. Assertiveness.

4. Sociability.

Couple traits:

1. Similarity.

2. Long acquaintanceship.

3. Good communication skills.

4. Good conflict resolution skills/style.

Context:
1. Older age.
2. Healthy family-of-origin experiences.
3. Happy parental marriage.
4. Parental and friends' approval.
5. Significant education and career preparation.

Remember that all of these factors are only indicators, not absolutes. Just because you have anxiety, a short acquaintanceship, or parental disapproval, that doesn't automatically mean that your marriage will fail. What matters most is what you do to keep it alive and happy. "With effort and commitment and caring," says Larson, your marriage can be a happy one. "Just don't expect it to be easy," he adds.

A secret technique. There is a Hawaiian expression that describes a technique that will guarantee a happy marriage: *hau'oli ke kekahi, hau'oli ka hale*, "happy spouse, happy house." Like many good techniques, it's very simple, but not very easy.

The concept is simple: keep your spouse happy, and the marriage will be happy. It's the application that's hard, because what makes your spouse happy, may not make you happy.

Some years ago I had a woman client who could not communicate with her husband. He was so different from her in interests and disposition that they didn't connect. In order to help her get closer to her husband I recommended a technique which involved her learning to walk like him and talk like him. After a month of this she reported that her husband was warming up to her, being more friendly and conversing more and apparently liking her more, but at the same time she was discovering that she really didn't like him as a person. She did get what she wanted, but then she decided that she didn't want what she got.

The "secret technique" works perfectly, but only if you are

willing to adapt. I'm not speaking of compromise, which in English implies giving up your principles to please someone else. That will never work well. But being willing to change some of your habits and attitudes and behaviors is absolutely necessary to making your marriage work. Life as a single person is not the same at all as life as a married person, just as life with a roommate is not the same as life with a spouse, quite apart from the sexual side of it. As my wife says, "You've got to give up the me for the we."

I have to admit that sometimes it feels like I'm giving up the me for the you, especially when I'm involved in a computer game and she wants me to take out the garbage, but those are little things that I can live with. What helps me adapt is that I have drastically reduced the number of things that I won't change, so that even though I might moan and grumble a bit at having to change a pattern of mine in favor of one of hers, it's almost always no big deal and I'll do it without resentment. What helps Gloria adapt is her willingness to tolerate a whole lot of my idiosyncrasies and to be willing to change her pattern when she encounters one of my few rock-solid ones.

Another man's solution that I read about was quite interesting. He said that in his family he made the big decisions and his wife made the little ones. He decided who should be President, what to do about global warming, and how to handle international relations, and she decided where they should live, how to raise the children, and what kind of car to buy.

If you always want it your way all the time, you are looking for a way to exert your power, not a way to express your love. A marriage, under those circumstances, becomes a sham, an excuse to have a legal servant and concubine, male or female.

If you are interested in a happy marriage, you might get

some inspiration from these definitions of the Hawaiian word for marriage, *ho'ao*, taken from the official marriage statement used for ceremonies in the Order of Huna International:

"Some idea of the meaning and intent of marriage can be had by noting these translations of the word *ao* : "to become enlightened; to take care of; to learn and to teach; to experience; a new shoot of taro (symbol of love); a team; a way of life; the *aumakua*." The word for "man" is *kane*, and the word for "woman" is *wahine*. The first can also be translated as the "breath of life" and the second as "the holder of life"."

In fact, I think the rest of the statement might be helpful, too, because in addition to some original thoughts it contains an adaptation of an excerpt from part of *The Prophet*, by Kahil Gibran:

"Aloha! We are gathered here to celebrate the union of this couple in marriage. It is a ceremony of commitment, and it is well to speak of the meaning of this commitment.

First, I would speak of love, and have you know that it is more than just a feeling that appears on some occasions and disappears on others. Rather, it is like a stream that ever flows yet never flows away.

It is the willing act of sharing your God-given life, of supporting one another in times of joy and sorrow, of cherishing, of helping one another to grow and blossom in fullness.

Ho'ao is the ancient Hawaiian word for marriage. The esteem in which marriage was held is indicated by the fact that the marriage ceremony always took place on the eleventh night of the old calender, the night called *Huna*.

Marriage is considered to be a commitment, yet not to each other. Marriage is not a state of mutual custody. Rather, it is a commitment to do certain things with and for each other. In this it follows, the Hawaiian word for "commit", *ho'oko*: "to fulfill; to succeed; to give support; partner-

200

ship; companion; strength." True marriage, then, is a commitment to love, to fulfill your lives together.

Let there be spaces in your togetherness, and let the winds of the heavens dance between you.

Love one another, yet make not a bond of love. Let it rather be a moving sea between the shores of your souls.

Fill each other's cup, yet drink not always from the same cup. Give one another of your food, but eat not always from the same bowl.

Sing and dance together and be joyous, yet let each one of you have your times alone, even as the strings of a guitar are alone, though they quiver with the same music.

Give your hearts, yet not into each others' keeping, for only the hand of Life can contain your hearts.

And stand together, yet not too near together. For the mountains of the islands stand apart, and the koa tree and the palm grow not in each other's shadow. Yet both the mountains and the trees stand on the same ground and reach toward the same sky.

It is good, then, to remember the unique identity of your soul, while knowing you are one in spirit."

Following this is the Marriage Vow:
"I commit myself to share my life with you; to cherish you; to support your success; to encourage your growth, and to increase your joy."

This chapter ends with another Hawaiian proverb about marriage:

He pili kua, he pili alo
Back to back and face to face
(a description of the marriage bond)

CHAPTER TEN
THE REST OF THE WORLD

This chapter will discuss relationships in general, including those that do not include parents, children, relatives, friends, lovers, or spouses. More techniques will also be presented that can apply to all kinds of relationships.

Masters and Slaves

This life is such an interesting experience. We are all participants in a vast game that we all agreed to play before we got here. The game consists in trying to thread our way between two worlds, each with a different set of rules. On the one hand, we have this three-dimensional physical world wherein we have to find food, shelter, clothing, companionship, and to confront other players of the game struggling to comprehend and cope. On the other hand, we have a, let us say, four-dimensional world which shows this reality to be a product of our own minds, an illusion, a "dream-world" from the fourth dimensional point of view.

What is the good of knowing all this? It depends on

whether you want to be a slave of life or its master. To be a slave of life is to accept everything around you as the ultimate reality and to act as if you have no control over it at all. It is to identify with the waves of energy that pass through you from time to time, which we call emotion, to think that they are you, that they are yours; and to let them condition your thinking, when in reality the energy was colored by your thinking in the first place. It is like a puppy chasing its own tail.

Then there is the problem of other people. Everything would be great if only they all did what you wanted or expected them to do. But other people are such contrary beings. Often they would rather do what they want, rather than what you want, even when you "know" that yours is the best way. So when they don't act according to our expectations and desires it upsets us terribly, causing emotional (energetic) trauma and feelings of helplessness and hopelessness. But—and consider this very carefully—when others don't act according to our desires and expectations, then perhaps something is wrong with our desires and expectations, and not with their behavior.

A slave of life is also terribly bound by material possessions like money, land, and goods. Their loss or lack causes emotional trauma and feelings of hopelessness and helplessness, too. We seek such "tangible" objects out of a need for security, but such a fragile and ephemeral type of security it is. The Bible parable of the man who worked his tail off for years and years to fill his barns and granaries with riches, only to find out on the very day that he thought he had attained material security that he was to depart this life the same night, reflects a fundamental truth. We are only passing through this life. The material world is only a tool for our experience. We are bound to suffer if we try to base our security on swirling atoms held in a temporary pattern, and to think of the pattern as the only reality.

The master of life—and it is the here-and-now potential of every human being to be such—knows that three-dimensional experience is a reflection of thought and no more. As a master of life you realize that you choose what you experience through your basic beliefs about life. You realize further, that to change your experience you have only to change your beliefs, and you understand the difference between desire and belief. You know that you, and only you, are responsible for all your happiness or unhappiness. And you also know one of the most important truths: that the way in which you experience life depends on how you choose to react to what happens to you. For this is an inborn, inalienable power that each of us has. We choose to be happy or sad, disgusted or overjoyed, impatient or understanding, bigoted or tolerant, inflexible or flowing. The slave chooses, too, but he lets his choice be determined by the will or acts of others, thus putting his power in their hands, and then he tries to blame others for his failure or unhappiness. The master of life chooses the way he wants to feel, to react, in terms of what will be the most effective for him, regardless of what happens.

I was extremely impressed with a short scene in the movie, "Matrix Revolutions." In this scene, the human hero, Neo, is fighting a titanic hand-to-hand battle with Mr. Smith, a humanoid computer program. Time after time Mr. Smith beats Neo to the ground, and time after time Neo gets back up to fight. Finally, after one battle sequence in which Neo is lying, apparently defeated, on the ground again, Mr. Smith speaks to him, using Neo's birth name:

Smith: "Why, Mr. Anderson, why? Why, why do you do it? Why, why get up? Why keep fighting? Do you believe you're fighting for something, for more than your survival? Can you tell me what it is, do you even know? Is it freedom? Or truth? Perhaps peace? Could it be for love? Illusions, Mr.

Anderson. Vagaries of perception. Temporary constructs of a feeble human intellect trying desperately to justify an existence that is without meaning or purpose. And all of them as artificial as the Matrix itself. Although, only a human mind could invent something as insipid as love. You must be able to see it, Mr. Anderson, you must know it by now! You can't win; it's pointless to keep fighting! Why, Mr. Anderson, why, why do you persist?"

Neo (getting up once again): "Because I choose to."

You are all, at all times, masters of your fate, insofar as your power to choose your reactions goes. The primary difference between the slave of life and the master of life is that the slave refuses to accept responsibility for his choices, and remains a slave, while the master of life chooses knowingly, and is free.

People speak of the courage that it takes to choose effectively, and of the struggle to choose one reaction over another. Actually, the only courage involved is that of risking someone else's displeasure at your choice. And the only struggle is against your own fear and doubt. Of course, it is easier to float than to swim; easier to go with the flow than to direct your course, but floating may bring you up against sharp and unpleasant rocks, while swimming brings you to safety.

To carry on the swimming analogy a bit, let us conceive of a particular experience in life as a rip tide. A rip tide is a strong current running from the shore out to sea a hundred yards or more. Let us use it to demonstrate a life experience over which you apparently have no control. Caught in the rip tide, a slave of life either panics and tries to struggle against the current, in which case he quickly loses his strength and drowns, or he gives up all hope and floats out to sea with the current, in which case he drowns anyway. The master of life, however, flows with the current until he feels its power weakening, and then he swims around it and back to shore. Both slave and master undergo the same experience. The difference is in how they react to it. To master life is not to control it; it is to master your relationship to it. A master surfer does not control the wave. He masters the art of riding it.

What Do You Want?

I often meet people who tell me that they don't know what they want, in terms of purpose, goals or relationships. My experience in helping such people over the years, however, has taught me that everyone knows what they want. It's just that some people are afraid to express it because they might not get it, and then they would feel bad. Daring to express what you want, even if it's only to yourself, increases your personal power and self esteem. Expressing what you want in a relationship can help to keep you out of a bad one, or help to heal an unhealthy one. First, though, you have to deal with the fear, and the Dynamind Technique is a wonderful resource for that. Here is one way in which it might be used for this problem:

1. Bring your fingertips together and take a deep breath.

2. Make a statement like this: "When I think of saying what I want I feel anxiety in my chest, and that can change. I want that feeling to go away."

3. Tap your chest, the upper web of both hands, and the base of your neck seven times each. Bring your fingertips back together.

4. Take a *piko-piko* breath by inhaling with your attention above your head and exhaling with your attention below your feet.

5. Think of saying what you want again and check how you feel. If necessary, repeat the process.

The Dynamind Technique can also be used to reinforce your ability to express what you want in a relationship. Here is how you might use it that way:

    1. Hold your hands as above.

    2. Make the statement: "I have the power to choose what I want, I have the right to choose what I want, I have the desire to choose what I want, I choose what I want right now."

    3. Tap as above.

    4. Breathe as above.

Knowing or deciding what you want in any encounter is highly useful, because it helps you to keep your focus on what's important, and keeps you from getting distracted by non-essentials. When I am working with clients, for instance, I always keep in mind what I want, which is to help them solve a problem. In order to be more effective in achieving what I want, I always ask the client what he or she wants at the beginning of the session. This helps both of us avoid endless talking about the problem and enables us to get right into solving the problem.

When you are involved in healing a relationship of any kind, keeping in mind what you want the healing to accomplish will help avoid digressions into power plays, blame and complaints, and criticisms as you move toward the healing.

Reconciliation

What do you do when there has been a break-up or estrangement from someone you care about? From time to time people ask me to bring a spouse or a lover or a friend back into their life after the person has left in anger or chosen someone else to be with. On occasion, in probing for motivations for the reconciliation, the client will say something like, "So he/she will crawl at my feet and beg for forgiveness!" Well, that's a client out the door. This kind of "reconciliation" is nothing but a desire for power and punishment, and it's no wonder the person left. Reconciliation can only occur when both people in a relationship have a good reason for getting back together. Ongoing feelings of hurt and anger can interfere with the good motivations, however, so here is a passive telepathic technique that has often proven successful. "Passive telepathy" is the act of broadcasting a mental message in such a way that the intended recipient has the free will to respond to it or not.

The Play Ball Technique. Although this is good for helping to reconcile friends, lovers, and spouses, it is also good for reconciling disagreements between parents and children, customers and clerks, or citizens and bureaucrats.

> 1. Imagine that you and the person you want to reconcile with are standing in an open field.
> 2. Imagine that you have a ball of some kind and start a game of tossing the ball back and forth.
> 3. Continue until the game is enjoyable and you feel better about the other person.

I have to tell you, sometimes this is very easy and sometimes it is very hard. I played ball with my father after he died and it seemed like he was trying to cause me injury rather than play ball. After a while of doing my best to avoid getting hit, I changed my framework (reinterpreted the action) to see it as him challenging me. Soon after that we had fun together and I felt that our relationship was healed in a way that it needed to be. Of course, in this case, the whole thing was symbolic of my feelings about my father, and not necessarily his feelings about me.

The following excerpt from my novel, Dangerous Journeys, describes two other examples of this technique, both taken from real-life situations. The scene begins after the hero, Keoki, has just alienated a new acquaintance:

"By this time he had stopped beating himself for being so rude and was trying to find a way to heal the situation. A plain apology would no doubt be politely accepted by Jeff, but it wouldn't improve their relationship. An abject apology would probably be received as a mockery. What could he do that would work? What would Gramps have done?

"Thinking of Gramps brought up a time when he was getting into a series of fights with another kid in grade school. He hadn't wanted to fight any more, but he couldn't think of any way to stop without breaking the other guys arms and legs. One evening Gramps had helped him to imagine that he was playing catch with his enemy. At the beginning of the imagination he and the other boy kept trying to bean each other with a baseball, but by the time Keoki finished some five minutes later he was imagining that they were tossing the ball back and forth in a friendly way. In school the next day the boy glared at him, but didn't try to start anything. Within a couple of days he even stopped glaring at Keoki. Within a couple of weeks they were playing football on the same team without any fuss. Keoki never became friends with the boy, but neither were they enemies any longer.

"What the heck, thought Keoki. What kind of ball do Britishers play? He thought of cricket, but he really didn't know much about the game. He knew they played rugby, but he also knew that it was a rough sport and that didn't seem appropriate. They also played soccer, he remembered. He would try that. In his mind he set up a soccer field where he and Jeff could practice. It took some effort to imagine Jeffrey in a soccer outfit, but he finally managed it. The next problem was that Jeff wouldn't play. Keoki would kick the ball to him, gently, and Jeff would simply fold his arms and look the other way. Keoki was stumped for a couple of minutes. Then he got the idea to turn the soccer ball into a globe of the earth. That got the imaginary Jeff's attention and with a little exertion of will Keoki was able to get the ball going back and forth quite nicely. When his image of Jeff started to smile Keoki figured it was enough for the time being."

Relationships With Events

Some of the most difficult kinds of events to relate to are war, disaster, and death. Here are some things I have written on these subjects.

Why is there war? People engage in war because they want to love or be loved. Although this may sound absurd at first, let's give it a closer look, because if we can understand the motivation for war then we might be able to redirect it.

The most fundamental human need is to be accepted, and the most fundamental fear is to be rejected. The old idea that survival comes first just doesn't hold up in the light of experience because it doesn't account for those who risk their lives for others, even strangers, and for those who commit suicide. And the fear of death is the fear of the ultimate rejection: by life itself.

Acceptance can be sought from oneself, one's environment (including people), or one's God, and many different strategies are used to ensure acceptance. If these strategies are pursued without fear, including fear-based anger, the result will be peace and cooperation. But as the fear of possible rejection increases, so does the tendency to seek acceptance by control or submission. Then the result is emotional repression, social suppression, and the use of violence to prove one's power or to make others accept oneself whether they want to or not.

In the case of war, the leaders who make the major decisions set standards to judge behavior by the "other side" as acceptable or unacceptable, motivated by their personal or group standards of self acceptance or acceptance from those around them. And those who obey the orders to march off to death and destruction are motivated by the desire to be accepted by doing "the right thing" or the fear of being rejected, and/or punished, for not doing it. What's so sad is that the fundamental intention is so good.

There is no glory in death and destruction. The so-called "glory" of war lies in the experience of incredible bravery, intense companionship, demonstrations of skill, the overcoming of limitations, successfully protecting one's country or loved ones, and the adulation for the winners. Yet, until we find a better way to satisfy the need for acceptance and the desire for real power, people will continue to go to war out of love.

Our great challenge, therefore, is not just to end war, but also to develop alternatives to war which still provide the benefits that only very intense experiences can generate, as well as satisfying the need for love.

A response to tragedy. When a great tragedy occurs the most natural thing to do for people with any degree of compassion is to want to help. If we are on the site we can plunge in with our minds and hearts and hands, like all the rescue workers, medical personnel and blood donors do. If we are not on site we can donate money to onsite helping organizations like the Red Cross and others, or we can pray for the victims and their friends and families. Still, none of this seems like enough and a sense of helplessness can move many people toward feelings of anger and retribution, or fear and confusion.

Let's give our desire to help a clear and effective focus. In addition to whatever else you feel is appropriate, let's give our prayers, energy, light, love, journeys and any other distant healing we can use to support the helpers, healers and peacemakers in the area of the tragedy who are working to assist those in pain and to resolve the problems caused by what has happened. Especially whenever a sense of helplessness arises, let us bless and strengthen their spirits and actions. Each time you become aware again of what happened and/or what's being done about it, here are some specific suggestions of what to do:

1. Pray to a higher power to help the helpers (which includes healers and peacemakers).

2. Imagine the helpers being surrounded by healing light and/or being assisted by angels or other spirit helpers.

3. If you know how, do an inner symbolic journey to help the helpers.

4. To the best of your ability, take the time to bring your own spirit to a state of peace by meditating on the beauty and goodness in the world, and practice positive expectation no matter what happens that the work of the helpers will be successful, in this world or another. This may be the most difficult thing of all to do ... and the most beneficial.

A Healing Circle

In my books, *Imagineering For Health* and *Urban Shaman* I give instructions for forming a "Healing Cooperative" and a "Kokua Group," respectively. These are both variations on the idea of a Healing Circle, which is just a group of people who want to join their minds and spirits for the benefit of others. Here is an easy way to do it, taken from the website of Aloha International:

1. Keep the organization simple. All you really need is someone to take responsibility for arranging and guiding the meetings.

2. Have regular weekly meetings if you can, because this helps to develop the healing power of the group. Otherwise, meet bi-weekly or at least once a month.

3. Three to seven people is a good size for a regular group, but it's fine if more people come from time to time. Let people come or not as they please. You do not need to turn it into a club or a class.

4. To begin, it's a good idea to harmonize your individual energies. The most simple way to do this is just to hold hands for a minute or two with your eyes closed and your attention on the feel of the hands. Even better is to add some time for everyone present to relate one good thing that has happened recently. Another good thing would be to let a volunteer lead a brief relaxing or inspirational meditation.

5. The next thing is to do some healing, for international, national, or local community problems; for people at a distance who have requested or need help; and for present members of the Circle. There are many techniques available for this in my books and those of others, or you may already know some. At Aloha International's Healing Circle on Kauai, members and visitors are invited to share different techniques with the group along with the more standard techniques that are used. The most important thing is to maintain the purpose as a Healing Circle, and not to let it become a class or a group therapy session.

Two Basic Distant Healing Techniques

The first one is called *La'a Kea*, "Lovelight," or "Clouds of Color." Everyone does the process silently.

1. Imagine yourself surrounded by a field of positive energy, in the form of light, color, sound, or vibration. Increase the intensity by *pikopiko* breathing (inhale at your crown, exhale below your feet) and/or thinking of happy memories.

2. Imagine this field expanding outward to include the person, place, or situation that you want to help.

3. Assume that this field of energy is responsive to your positive intentions, and give it instructions on

how you want it to be helpful. Use simple directions like "Enlighten!" "Release!" "Focus!" "Center!" "Bless!" "Empower!" or "Assist!"

The second one is a variation on The Dynamind Technique.

1. Have someone name a person, place, or situation that you want to help.

2. Make a statement like this all together: "There is a problem and that can change. We want that problem to go away, we want the condition/situation to be healed."

3. All together, make seven taps of your fingertips on the center of your chest, on the web part of each hand, and on the bone at the base of your neck. Then finish with a *pikopiko* breath.

After the group does a healing together it's always a good idea for everyone to share their experience of the process. This not only reinforces the bond of the group, it also helps the members of the group learn from each other's experiences.

Aloha a hui hou - "Love until we meet again"

And so the relationship between author and reader comes to a point of departure. It seems only fitting to me, naturally, that I leave you with another proverb:

Hauʻoli ke aloha, he kilohana e paʻa ai
Love is a joyful thing, the best of all to hold onto

About The Author

Serge Kahili King, Ph.D. has authored many books, audio presentations, and videos based on Hawaiian culture and the philosophy of Huna. He is a member of Phi Beta Kappa and holds degrees Asian Studies, Foreign Trade, International Management, and Psychology. His unconventional education includes having apprenticed to Hawaiian and African shamans, and having studied with shamans from Mongolia, Siberia, Finland, and Mexico.

Dr. King lives in Hawaii with his wife, Gloria, and is the Executive Director of Aloha International, a worldwide network of people dedicated to doing their best to make the world a better place.

Those interested in learning more about Dr. King's teachings and the work of Aloha International are invited to visit:

The Hawaiian Huna Village - www.huna.org
The Aloha Project - www.alohainternational.org
The Huna Store - www.huna.net

CPSIA information can be obtained
at www.ICGtesting.com
Printed in the USA
LVOW10s0820260817
546480LV00001B/13/P